FUTURE POETS

"A Guide For Aspiring Writers"

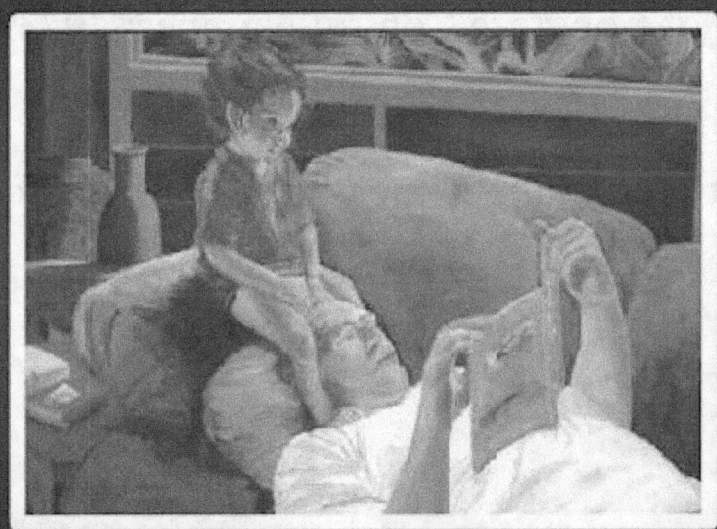

ROD MARTIN

Teachers should be free to copy poems and lists of suggestions to give out to the students or to study for oral presentations.

ISBN: 978-1-961677-86-9 (Paperback)
ISBN: 978-1-961677-23-4 (E-book)

Library of Congress Control Number: 2023915618

Printed in the United States of America

Published by:

info@thequippyquill.com
(302) 295-2278

Future Poets

By Rod Martin

(A writing guide for aspiring poets)

For Emily and Julia
who keep me writing poems

Future Poets Contents:

Poetry Challenges:

Dedication:

This book is for all my fellow teachers out there who enjoy poetry and believe their students will become better writers if they keep practicing. Kids so often just need something interesting and challenging to write about: that is how this book can help.

Here are hundreds of ideas to stimulate your student's imaginations; students who are often willing to write, but don't have a clue what to write about. These ideas will give them a place to start.

Poetry, with its conciseness, emotion, and lack of punctuation is a great way to begin each school year and ease the kids into other forms of writing.

Poetry lends itself to success. Anyone can do it. And it's personal; it comes from the students' experiences and emotions. It's subjective; the sort of writing to be appreciated rather than judged.

It's my hope that your students will come to enjoy writing more after having tried these poetry ideas that give them a variety of choices and challenges.

Yo, poets
Listen up
The president
Barack Obama said:

When we have faced down impossible odds;
(finishing this poetry challenge)
When we've been told that we're not ready,
(what do kids know about poetry?)
Or that we shouldn't try,
(who says I can't do this?)
Or that we can't,
(I'm no quitter)
Generations of Americans
(And I'm one)
Have responded with a simple creed
That sums up the spirit of a people:

Yes, we can.

Here's a poem I like to read to my students at the start of our poetry unit:

> I write this to read this to you kids to say
> I'm thankful you're here, kids
>   This could be the day
>   I reach you and teach you
>   to find your own voice
>
> You've got the chance
>   You make the choice
>
> There's a world of ideas
>   bouncing 'round in your head
> and when you write them down, so they can be read
>   then others might know what you're feeling inside
> and they too will write
>   and then know the pride
>   of sharing a moment
>   or speaking their heart
> Just put pen or pencil on paper:
>   that's where it starts
> There's a kind of magic
>   the way words paint a scene
> Do you get the picture?
>   Do you understand what I mean?
> There's a joy to creating
>   To making something new
> I hope you'll enjoy writing
>   Because your writing's a part of you.

What is poetry?

Webster's New World Dictionary

tells us that a poem is:

An arrangement of words
Written or spoken
A rhythmical composition
Sometimes rhymed
Expressing experiences,
Ideas or emotions
In a style more concise,
imaginative, and powerful
than ordinary speech or prose

(That it is

and so much more)

Why Poetry

Poetry works well for engaging student writers because it is challenging and yet flexible. There are so many types and styles of poems they can experience. There's also a lot of leeway in terms of punctuation, idioms and slang, and how the words appear on the page.

The emphasis in this book is students as poets. It's not about studying the famous poets who have gone before. It's about finding a love for expressing yourself that can last a lifetime.

It's my hope that this book will help your students come to a better understanding of poetry and eventually feel confident in their ability to write poetry.

Structuring Your Poetry Unit

May I suggest calling your poetry assignments "Poetry Challenges". That way, it seems more like a game or competition. It's not a matter of who has the best poem, but "can you do this?" the challenge is to fulfill the criteria for that particular poem, not always create a great literary work. Poets throughout time have had to communicate their ideas following certain rhythmic and rhyme patterns.

These challenges are the same sort of thing. Can you say what you want to say, clearly, without letting the criteria get in your way.

I recommend starting the school year with poetry until you feel the students have a good grasp of poems and poetic devices.

I have put Poetic Devices after the Poetry Challenges, but I recommend the teacher choose one of these concepts every other day. Once the students are comfortable with Poetic Devices, you should see them using them in their Poetry Challenges.

For the rest of the year, give them as least one weekly poetry challenge. This will add a bit of variety to their work while maintaining the continuity and familiarity with concepts covered in the initial poetry unit.

Poetry Challenges

It's All About Me…

Finish the following phrases for an Autobiographical Poem that will let others know some interesting and new things about you:

I am…

I want…

I believe…

I will not…

I hope…

I dream…

I'm saddened by…

I hate…

I remember…

I would love…

<u>Five Finger Poetry:</u>

These poems have only five words. It's easy because it's so short. The challenge is to say a lot with only five words: that means being concise.

There are two styles: "Sentence Style" which sounds like someone speaking and "Words on a Topic Style" which are like snapshots that fit together to make a complete picture.

<u>Examples of Sentence Style:</u>

You can express yourself poetically.

Five finger poems are short.

Take the time to rhyme.

I'd be blue without you.

I can't think of anything.

<u>Examples of "Words on a Topic Style"</u>

Tackling, passing, running, scoring, cheers.

Spark, Flame, Curtains, Crib, Sirens.

Waves, Swimming, Surfing, Diving, Fishing.

Pitch, hit, run, slide, score!

<u>Some Possible Topics for Student Five Finger Poems:</u>

<u>Love:</u>

You take my breath away.

Your breath keeps me away.

I love loving only you.

Your smile lifts my heart.

Love me with your eyes.

Love can set you free.

Love can be so complicated

I love you so much

Hugs, kisses, sighs, your eyes

Flirting, talking, embracing, arguing, crying

Nature:

Our mountains are so amazing

The ocean gives us life

Huge waves pound the shore

The beach is our playground

Sun, sand, surf, friends, paradise

School:

I'm a life long learner

Lunch is my favorite subject

Ignorance will get you nowhere

Knowledge has no limits ever

I like going to school

Loud, rhythm, percussion, drumline, band

Teachers, lessons, socializing, learning, laughing.

Preschool, elementary, intermediate, high school

Friends:

I cherish all my friends

My friends keep me sane

My friends make me laugh

I couldn't live without friends

Shopping, sleepovers, phoning, secrets, crushes

Beliefs:

I believe love lasts forever

I believe in Aloha's power

Love is the best emotion

Never hate, steal or kill.

Faith, family, church, songs, praise.

Temple, tradition, Torah, Hebrew, Hosannah

Family:

My family is my treasure

Family is there for me

You just can't fool mom.

Cute, small, soft, fragile, baby

Fights, fun, meals, vacations, madness

Emotions: (love, hate, fear, sorrow, joy, hurt)

I hate how hate feels.

I fear living all alone

Loss wraps us in sorrow

You bring me such joy

Heartbreak, confusion, tears, time, healing

The Senses: (sight, touch, smell, hearing and taste)

To see you is heaven.

Scarred from mom's tongue lashing

Butter dipped lobster so sweet.

<u>Advanced work:</u> Take your favorite five finger poem and expand it into a longer piece.

<u>Some student examples:</u>

movies, shows, comedy, romance, television

music makes me wanna dance

Bumping, hitting, blocking, jumping, volleyball

Summer is the best ever

Please don't read this poem.

Eat, sleep, school, work, play

I wish I was rich.

Blood, death, guns, stupid war.

Peace power to the people.

I like to travel places

Imaginative, realistic, mysterious, action, books

Baby, it's all about me

Adjective Poems

Have students fill in the blanks in the following poem with adjectives. Rewriting the poem a few times with differing adjectives will show the students how important descriptive words are to the overall meaning of any poem.

The_____man

    Had_____words for the woman

She looked_____.

His_____eyes told_____stories

And her_____expression spoke louder than words.

The filthy man
Had drunken words for the woman
She looked disgusted
His bleary eyes told heartbreak stories
And her frightened expression spoke louder than words.

The wealthy man
Had romantic words for the woman
She looked delighted
His kind eyes told thrilling stories
And her amused expression spoke louder than words

Fill in the Blank Poems

Have your students use the following structure to create a variety of poems. Tell them to avoid trying to rhyme. Perhaps they can come up with some real surprises.

In your eyes I've seen_____

    Touched_____

    Felt_____

But_____

    So_____

In your eyes I've seen starlight
Touched sorrow
Felt sunshine
But tears don't belong in such dreams
So dry your eyes and reflect only love from now on.

In your eyes I've seen Volkswagens
Touched chrome
Felt the power of your acceleration
But you drive too fast
So remember me when you need to refuel your love.

Another "Fill in the Blank Poem":

I'm asking you_____

Don't tell me_____

I've seen you_____

But never_____

If you don't_____

Then I'll_____

And you can_____

I'm asking you to call me
Don't tell me you don't like me because I know you do
I've seen you looking at me
But never thought you'd ever really care
If you don't call, I'll be heart broken
Then I'll tell all my friends what a jerk you can be
And you can eat lunch all by yourself

I'm asking you to love me more
Don't tell me I'm too theatrical
I've seen you be flirtatious
But never thought you'd want someone else
If you don't need this love of ours
Then I'll surely set you free
And you can learn to love again in someone else's arms.

Haiku

Haiku is a form of poetry from Japan.
It's very short and fairly easy to write
It doesn't rhyme. It has only three lines that are all about one subject.

In the short form, the first line has three syllables, the second line has five syllables, and the third line has three syllables. (3-5-3)

The long form has five syllables in the first line, the second line has seven syllables, and the third line has five syllables. (5-7-5)

Example: Short form

3 Maturing
5 Anticipating
3 Destiny

Long Form

5 Shining waterfall
7 Slithering down the mountain
5 Filling a blue pool

Haiku Short Form examples:

I can't think

This is just too hard

I give up

Pain, blood, gore.
Why must there be war?
No one wins.

Island breeze
Bringing sweet relief
From the heat

Please love me
I'm so lonely lost
Ease this pain

They tease me
But can't see the hurt
Hidden tears

Haiku Long Form Examples:

I love my reggae
Skankin' to that reggae beat
I could dance 'till dawn

The morning sunshine
Enters through the window's glass
Past dust and cobwebs

You changed my whole world
When you told me you loved me
You've made me complete

Count on your fingers
You just count the syllables
Your haiku is done

School Pride Haikus

Our school, very cool
We never ever give up
We all can stand proud

This school is awesome
We are very respectful
And responsible

Our school is the best
I love attending this place
And you should also

This is a good school
Because of all the people
Let's keep it that way

The Poetry of "If"

These are simple poems that have a distinct rhythm, just three
or four lines and only one rhyme

If I was a cloud
And you were the sky
Would you smile at me as I pass on by?

If I was a flower
And you were a tree
Would you share your shade
and grow by me?

If I were insecticide
And you were a roach
I might have to kill you when you approach

If I were your teacher
And you were my class
You'd have to work hard
if you wanted to pass

Acrostic Poems

These poems focus on just one word (your name, topic, or concept) written in bold print down the page, with words or sentences about that topic, starting with the letters that make up that word.

Example:

A rtists show us ourselves and our world
R eact differently to the world around them
T ry to inspire us
I admire their ability to create new ideas
S ee things others miss
T ell us how it can be, not just how it is.

Create an Acrostic Poem using your first name. Remember that every sentence must start with one of the letters of your name and must be about you.

Examples of name acrostics:

Ridiculous and ready to laugh
Only does what he likes to do
Doesn't give up easily

Japanese American upbringing
Anchor for our family
Never idle
Easy to love

Eager to try new things
My darling grand-daughter
I love this little one
Laughs easily
Yes she's my only and only favorite

Create an Acrostic Poem (or several) from the following words:

Freedom, Hope, Surfing, Guitar, Friends, Family, Skateboarding, Nature, Truth, Unique, Love, Dating, Crush, Eating, Hiking, Biking, Ocean, Hawaii, Swimming, Power, Pride, Mountains, Sailing, Diving, Heartbreak, Resilient, Imagination, Beach, Racing, Shopping, Liberty, Honesty, Laughter, Sorrow, Band, Paradise, Sunshine, Lost, Lonely, Brothers, Sisters, Mom, Dad, Grandma, Grandpa, Uncle, Auntie, Flowers, Rain, Sunshine, Storms, Wind, Rivers, Mistakes, Dreams, Heroes, Fame, Food, Forgotten, Jealous, Twisted, Forgiveness, Pain, Traveling, America, Earth, Rumors, Relationships, Celebrate, or suggest a word of your own choosing.

Acrostic Poem Examples

SCHOOL

S-ometimes it's fun and sometimes it isn't

C-ould we have a longer lunch, please?

H-ave teachers forgotten what it's like to be kids?

O-nly friends make it interesting

O-n hot days, we melt into our seats

L-et's try to make it more exciting

PAIN

P-lease make the hurting stop

A-ll I can think about is the pain

I-n agony over you

N-ever break my heart like that again

Make

All

The

Homework easy to understand

Family are

Always there for

Me

If I need

Love from someone other than

You

Friendly

Respectful

Independent

Energetic

Nice

Dependable

Special

Super angry

Tremendously mad

Rising emotion

Easily infuriated

Snappy attitude

Strangely upset

Drift into a world where

Reality doesn't

Exist

And you're in a place where your

Mind

Sleeps without waking 'til morning

My mom is

Outstandingly

Magnificent in many ways

Quatrains

A quatrain is any four line poem that rhymes. The second and fourth lines always rhyme; the first and third lines may or may not rhyme. The rhymed lines should contain approximately the same number of syllables.

Like lighthouses among the trees
Fireflies glitter on quiet nights
Fearful of kids and a strong breeze
Darting about sharing their light

I'm a crazy teenager
But I'll make it somehow
This life is for the living
And I must live mine now

Listen to the rhythm
Don't get caught up in the rhyme
It's just a little poem
To help you pass the time

If you want to write a quatrain
It's an easy thing to do
Like the sound of the falling rain
Then put in a piece of you

Autobiographical Cinquain

1) On the first line, write your name or nickname.
2) On the second line, write two words that describe you
3) On the third line, write three things you like to do
4) On the fourth line, write a sentence you believe to be true about life.
5) On the fifth line, write another version of your name.

Mr. Rod
Optimistic and theatrical
Singing, writing, adventuring
Look for the loving thing to do
Rodaroo

Cinquain About Anything

1) On the first line, write the noun you want to describe.
2) On the second line, write two words that describe that noun
3) On the third line, write three verbs (action words) that relate to that noun.
4) On the fourth line, write a sentence about that noun
5) On the fifth line, write about why that thing is important

Water
Delicious, essential
Falling, flowing, freezing
I love to be one with water
Without it, we would surely die.

Diamantes

A Diamante is a seven line poem in a diamond shape that contrasts two different things. Opposites work well. Center each line on the paper. 1.) The first line is just one noun, the first subject. 2.) The second line is just two adjectives that describe the first subject. 3.) The third line is three verbs that relate to the first subject. 4.) The fourth line is four nouns, the first two nouns relating to the first subject and the second two nouns relating to the final subject (or opposite of the first subject). 5.) The fifth line is three verbs relating to the final subject. 6.) The sixth line is two adjectives that describe the final subject. 7.) The seventh line is one noun, the final subject.

School

Challenging, Exciting

Learning, Experimenting, Socializing

Homework, Examinations, Relaxation, Freedom

Playing, Traveling, Cruising

Warm, Marvelous

Vacation

Peace

Calm, Safe

Playing, Traveling, Relaxing

Families, Friends, Enemies, Terrorists

Destroying, Killing, Conquering

Deadly, violent

War

Free Verse

Free verse breaks all the rules. It's free. It can have any sort of pattern. It may contain rhyme or assonance but it doesn't have to. The rhythms can vary. Words and phrases can be put in any position on the page. (I like to group thoughts together, but occasionally have something stand alone for emphasis) It's experimental. Students will be relieved to know that this is one kind of poetry that's hard to do wrong. Sometimes they need to be reminded to keep things appropriate for the school setting (it's not that free) by avoiding swearing or writing something hurtful about one of their peers.

Betty Sue of Tuscaloo
        walks along the railroad tracks
            that pass through her small town

Looking down and remembering the young man, Dan
        who passed through her life
                          her town
                              her love

He came to build a school
        He left to fight a war a world away

And when came the day
        that train brought him back
            as he stood there beside the track
                Betty Sue instinctively knew
                    that the love she once had come to know
                        had died in a battle not so long ago

And only a body here remained
        to carry around the living pain
            like the lonesome moan of a passing train

Shout This Poem

I travel at the speed of poetry

Moving though time

Free

To rhyme of ramble

I roam about

I sing this poem

I laugh

I shout this poem to the stars

Such sweet release

A poem for peace

In this world of ours

Grown up?

An impossible feat.

No one ever really grow up.

We're still kids

Playing different games

Still harboring the same fears.

I've been growing up for years

I wish I could start growing down

I like those younger games better.

Starting Line Poems

Ask your students to write on a piece of scratch paper (recycled) three possible starting lines for a poem. Have them pick their favorite of the three and write it on the board. To save time, the teacher may hand out a list of starting lines. Each student then picks a starting line that he or she likes and writes a poem of at least ten lines. It does not need to rhyme: ideas are what's important. For a variation, you can have the whole class begin with the same starting line and see how differently things turn out. The same thing can be accomplished with small groups using the same beginning and then reading their poems to each other.

Starting Lines for Poems

Spreading the joy...

When I go out, I like to hang with my friends...

I like to lie in the grass and look up at the clouds...

Summer days just sitting around, but when the sun goes down…

I am very competitive...
Crash and burn…

Going down the hill on my skateboard feeling the wind whipping through my shirt...

The door to another world opened...

A book can take you anywhere at any time...

I like to spend quality time with my family and friends...

I wish I was running on the grassy field …

When I'm with my brother, I'm free...

Mother, there's a monster under my bed…

The sound of a heartbreak...

I like to be happy, even giggling is fun...

The bright moon...

When I imagine things it's like I'm in a dream...

Love the beach...

I like video games with lots of action...

I have been waiting for your love...

I like to listen to the sound of a water fall...

Go ride some waves...

I would like to go back to the past...

I have no bedtime...

Walking on the moon...

On Sundays my mind travels everywhere...

My mother kills a part of me when she yells at me...

I knew you were always there...

I see rainbow bubbles that burst into clear air...

You don't need weed to succeed...

When you're near, I get a joyful feeling in my heart...

My Dad is the greatest...

Somehow our hearts collided together and became one...

Traveling the galaxy, exploring new planets...

Reaching my goals...

Death really messes things up...

Eyes glued to the TV, can't move...

Flying, watching clouds pass by...

Being grounded...

The calming sensation of an afternoon nap...

Jumping off a high cliff into the water makes my heart beat so fast...

Life would be so sweet if...

Music, so cool...

Dreams are weird...

My parents shower me with gifts...

Kids playing football...

Swimming, the cold water on water in my skin...

I love my mom...

Flowers, flowers, everywhere...

I hate to have nightmares...

Heartbreak is a headache...

I love to talk...

Stars are so awesome...

Bombs dropping through the smoke of war...

I like to rhyme all the time...

When school is done, it's time for fun...

Just me and my music...

I've seen what drugs can do to you...

I don't like rumors...

I have my dad's credit card in my pocket and I'm going shopping...

Jealousy can be a bad thing...

I don't like seeing blood...

My mom and dad are my heroes...

There's nothing like opening presents on Christmas day...

I hate rainy days...

New born babies are so cute...

I love looking at the mountains...

There's nothing like a cherry-filled glazed donut...

I will always remember my younger days...

I hate people who tease me...

I like to dream…

That's funny, you don't seem like that type to me.

I'm in a great deal of pain.

I guess you're darned if you do, and darned if you don't.

Someone should call the police!

I can't believe I'm doing this.

I don't want to hear another word.

Did I hear what I think I heard?

It's so romantic, isn't it?

This could be dangerous.

I have a confession to make.

How do I know you're really my friend?

Homework is not an option.

I'll I-M your I-Pod if you text mess my Blueberry.

There's got to be a better way.

Starts With a Question

Is there homework for the homeless?

Why do we have dreams?

Why are people mean?

Why do we have rules?

Why do we have wars?

Why is everyone different?

Who am I?

Are you born with the talent to sing or dance?

Is there a pollution solution…

Is watching TV bad for you?

Why do we have emotions?

How do you know what is true?

Does everybody fall in love?

Why are we here?

Will we ever run out of drinkable water?

What was your favorite toy?

What makes you angry?

What would you change about yourself?

What would you like to tell your parents?

What gives you stress?

Where is your favorite place on earth?

If you could be some other living creature, what would you choose to be?

Who's your hero?

How would your friends describe you?

What hurts your feelings?

If you could change just one thing in this world, what would it be?

Can your brain get full?

Poems by the Topic

Have your students pick a topic from the following list or come up with a topic of their own. I usually ask them to write at least ten lines. They can rhyme if they like, do free verse or experiment with the styles they've been learning. If you feel the students require some guidance, have them first write the name of the topic and any other names it may have, then describe it using the five senses, then try to compare it to something else (simile or metaphor), and finally, ask them to express a personal feeling, idea, or memory about the topic. You can always ask them to include some alliteration or repetition in the piece to keep them aware of the various poetic devices.

Topics for Poems

Wind, Rain, Sand, War, Peace, Earth, Friends, Fun, Music, Swimming, Bikes, Toys, Skating, Fear, Love, Sorrow, Joy, Pain, Loss, Holidays, Water, Heaven, Clouds, Computers, Acting, Fighting, Teachers, Parents, Relatives, Travel, Animals, Sports, Players, Television, Movies, Art, Technology, Internet, History, Heroes, Sunsets, Sun, Flowers, Gifts, Jealousy, Anger, Space, Confusion, Exhaustion, Power, Beaches, Hurricanes, City Lights, Halloween, Christmas, Summer, Sailing, Diving, Hate, Work, Honesty, Wild Animals, Accidents, Being Grounded, Nightmares, Snow, Sight, Churches, Lightning, Blood, Cars,

Airplanes, Sickness, Golf, Cartoons, Paddling, Ninjas, Waterfalls, Dirt Bikes, Donuts, Tennis, Boys, Girls, Ghosts, Death, Witches, Faith, Skateboarding, Rock and Roll, Gothic Style, Memories, Stars, Movie Stars, Money, Monsters, Happiness, Sorrow, Jealousy, Cheer leading, Hurts, Babies, Goals, Resiliency, Responsibility, Respect, Pollution, Resourcefulness, Reading, Bed Time, Rap, Volley Ball, Fruit, Hiking, Kayaking, Fishing, Camping, Praying, Meditating, Heartbreak, Headaches, Hamsters, Dentists, Clouds, Fire, Eating, Texting, Games, Sports, Embarrassing Moments, Mistakes, The Cosmos, Space Travel, Jobs, America, Cities, Country Living, Boredom, Hope, Grief, Time, Heartbreak, Silliness, Jokes, Pranks, Aging, Relatives, The Future, Thanks, Forgiveness, Global Warming, Pollution, Terrorists, Questions, Driving, Fireworks, Failure, Deforestation

(And of course, you can always write on a topic of your own choosing.)

If the topic were city lights:

There's a river of lava light

That flows from the mountains to the sea

From Honolulu to Waikiki

And though it's only streetlights, right…

Like Pele's fire

Progress consumes everything

In its path

Perhaps we will be known as the creatures

Who prefer light

At night

If the topic were religion:

Inhale

Every breath

    Every conscious breath

        Can be a meditation, of sorts

            Sniffs and snorts of mother air

Which we hardly appreciate

    Until it's not there

        for a minute or two

If only our love for God and each other

    Could become as indispensable

            As air.

If the topic were trees:

Banyan

Banyan
Reaches out
Overhangs
> Begs to be climbed

Big
> Shade casting
>> Roots swinging

Castle tall
> Rainbow wide

Massive toadstool of greenery
> Tree trunk scenery

Wind resistant
> Earth clutching
>> Cluster of growth

Night time condominium for birds

Mother earth mushroom climbing cloud

If the topic was loneliness:

Most Alone

The most alone thing

Is waking up

To the same thing you saw

When you went to sleep

And it only has one eye

That cannot see you, you see?

It's your TV.

Emotion Poems

Pick an emotion (Love, Fear, Joy, Sorrow, Grief, Surprise, Jealousy, Hatred, Disgust, etc.) and answer the following questions about it. You may answer them in any order. If a question doesn't fit, leave it out. Don't forget to end with a strong concluding statement about that emotion.

Where does it live?
What is it saying to you?
What does it feel like?
How does it sound?
What does it look like?
What would it wear?
What would you like to say to it? (put these lines in quotation marks)
What does it taste like?
How does it make you feel?

End with a concluding statement that sums up your ideas and feelings about this emotion.

Hatred

Hatred lives inside us
Churning our guts
Burning in our brains
It's evil words spat out in anger
Like mom yelling about my grades
It's a raging fire
A punch to the face
A wooden spoon to my backside
Hatred hurts like a tension headache
      trying to burst out my skull
"Hatred, you're killing me."
You wear a red face,
      a terrorist's mask
You listen for revenge with evil ears
You tell me to lash out
You leave my dry mouth tasting of ashes
I hate hatred

Loneliness

So boring
  So depressing
Emptiness
  Isolation
Loneliness wears stuffy,
  long sleeves and dresses all in blue
It lives under a quiet railroad bridge,
  and in mental hospitals,
    in crowded schools,
  and dark cramped attics of emptiness
It's tasteless and dry
"Loneliness, I don't want you!"
It tells me, "You're locked up forever."
In a dark corner,
an old person stands with no shadow
Looking like nobody I need to know
It's no life to live.

Happiness

Feels like new clothes out of the dryer.
Sounds like Christmas morning
Opening presents and
    it's what you always wanted
Crinkle, crumple,
    ripping of wrapping paper.
The oven timer beeping to say
    the pie is done.

Happiness wears bright colors
It's a cool swimming pool
    on a hot day

I would say, "I love you.
    Don't ever go away."

It's saying to you,
"I will give you joy and happiness."

Jealousy

Jealousy lives in a nicer house than me.
Making me feel poor.
I want what they have.
It says I am not good enough.
Watching those two flirt,
It's quicksand.
It stops me.
A black hole that keeps pulling me in.
A slap in my face.
Jealousy, something I don't want to feel
     but everybody does.
Like a migraine that doesn't go away.
Jealousy. "Why doesn't she like me?"
It wears a dark black robe
     and has sharp nails
Its shadow's even better than me.
A fear inside me
I don't want to feel jealousy!

Riddle Me This

There is a hell
    we know so well
        that dwells within us
all the same

It cuts and kills
    breaks our will
        even before we know its name

We try to hide
    shove it aside
        and find someone to blame

Our hurt
    our lies
        We criticize
            trying to survive the game

If we're no good
    perhaps we should
        learn to deal with shame.

Grief

You're in a better place

You lived there since you were seven

You have a new address

and it's right up in heaven

you used to like sunny days

rainy days as well

you laughed when you got tickled

you even laughed when you fell

You told me you had dreams

of reaching the stars

and about going to all the planets

especially Mars

You wanted big achievements

You had many goals

You left me in sorrow

but you're still in my soul

I'm praying every night

Hoping you're okay

I'll be with you again

in heaven someday.

Limericks

The rhyme scheme for limericks is A,A,B,B,A. The first, second, and fifth lines are longer and have three strong beats. The third and fourth lines are shorter and have two strong beats. It's fun to scat sing (Da, da's) the rhythm and emphasis of the beats and also gives the students an idea of just how many words can fit into the pattern of a Limerick.

Some of my students like to cruise

But I tell them if you snooze, you lose

Challenge you mind

Get off your behind

And try your best: what do you choose?

There was a young fellow from Perth

Who was born on the day of his birth

He was married, they say

On his wife's wedding day

And he died when his soul left the earth

A limerick is easy to do

After the first line comes number two

The third is a breeze

The fourth comes with ease

And the last line is all up to you

Marginal Poetry

This style of poetry began when I used to write little poems in the margins of my notebooks, when I should have been paying better attention in class. You try to say a lot with very few words, words stacked one atop the other. For advanced work, predetermine how many words the students may use; like a dozen.

Read

This	Rainy	run
Now	Day	walk
You	Runs	jump
Read	Down	hop
A	window	fly
Piece	my	roll
of	pain	jog
Poet	framed	skip
before	in	trip
you	broken	meander
know	glass	to
It	heart	school

Ends

Metaphor

The easiest way to describe something is to compare it to something else.   That's all a metaphor really is, just a comparison. If night was falling, one could call it a "curtain of stars" approaching.   You could call the football teams' huge blocker "a brick wall" and that's a metaphor. You just don't use the words 'Like' or 'As' because that turns a metaphor into a Simile.

I use the fill in the blank poem "My Country 'tis a Ship" to start things rolling.   It uses a sailing ship metaphor to describe America.

Metaphor Poem

Write the line and then chose one of the options to fill in the blank or come up with your own.

My country 'tis a ship,
Sailing on _____
(global seas, troubled waters, oily seas, stormy seas, waves of terror)
Crewed by _____
(people from all nations, people of diversity, you and me)
Bourne on the winds of _____
(freedom, change, war)
Kept afloat by _____
(military might, our hopes and dreams, inflated dollars)
Seeking safe harbor_____
(in a place of peace, in the constitution, in freedom's future)
On this journey to_____
(freedom's shore, our future, our nation's destiny)

<u>Metaphor Challenge</u>: pick one of the following and write a poem making as many comparisons as you can between the two topics:

Learning as a car ride

Your brain as a computer

Earth as a mother

Television as a teacher

Life as a road

War as a chicken fight

Work as a race

Love as a sport

Your school as a food

School as a video game

Romance as a computer virus

Metaphor example: <u>Life as a Road</u>

Life is a road with many different routes to choose from.

It has its ups and downs

You must go at your own speed

      and there is often something in your way:

Stoplights are telling you to stop and look at things

      from a different perspective

SUV obstacles and Traffic Jams are dreams delayed.

The back roads can be pathways to new opportunities

      or sidetracking trouble like drugs or crime

Oh, yes, Life's road has many twists and turns

One big curve is marriage (talk about changing lanes!)

Detours are when you're sick or injured.

Intersections are decisions.

If there are bumps in the road, don't let them stop you

Pay attention to where you're going

Don't get distracted

like someone talking on their cell phone while driving

And keep in mind, in the end, we all have to exit.

An intersection as a metaphor for life's decisions:

Welcome to the crossroads, kid
The start and end of everything
You ever did
Here, decisions run in different directions
That way or this
Depression or bliss
What road you on, kid?
Slip, slide or skid
Dash, crash or cruise
Life lets you choose
Dreamer or schemer
Grouch, slouch, or couch potato
Which way you gonna go?
Fast, slow, high, low
Or just sit and sing the blues
You gotta choose
Blues are a reason to sing
Isn't it all just how you look at a thing?

Population concerns compared to illness metaphor:

Over-population is a disease
Over time
Over population
In every town, place and nation
Our planet has a virus
                    and it's us
Fast-spreading and deadly
With weapons of concrete
                        Prolific procreation
More all the time
        More than ever before
                How many more will it take
'Till Earth breaks
        Gives in
                Gives out?

Poor little planet with a bad case

                of humanity

Metaphor poem comparing flowers and love:

Love is a flower

So let it bloom

Plant the seed

And give it room

Believe in the flower

Without any doubt

Water it daily

And watch it sprout

Be gentle and patient

And take it slow

And you will see how beautiful

Love will grow

Nothing More Than Feelings

Poems so often express how we feel. Choose from the following list of feelings to create a poem that rhymes or at least has some rhyming words (assonance) in it. Ten line minimum.

Amazed, Afraid, Annoyed, Apathetic, Alarmed, Ashamed, Amused, Affectionate, Angry, Anxious, Bashful, Brave, Bored, Bewildered, Calm, Curious, Confused, Cautious, Confident, Crushed, Daring, Delighted, Desperate, Doubtful, Defeated, Disgusted, Depressed, Devastated, Disliked, Dejected, Disappointed, Discouraged, Disturbed, Eager, Envious, Exhausted, Embarrassed, Frustrated, Fearful, Frantic, Fed Up, Friendly, Furious, Frightened, Glad, Grateful, Guilty, Gloomy, Grieving, Grouchy, Happy, Hopeless, Humiliated, Horrified, Hurt, Helpless, Hostile, Hopeful, Humbled, Impatient, Independent, Infatuated, Irritated, Important, Indifferent, Inferior, Insecure, Inhibited, Insulted, Jealous, Jittery, Lazy, Loyal, Lost, Lustful, Loved, Lonely, Mad, Mischievous, Moody, Miserable, Nervous, Nosey, Optimistic, Overwhelmed, Peaceful, Panicked, Pressured, Puzzled, Proud, Pessimistic, Patient, Relieved, Regretful, Restless, Relaxed, Say, Sexy, Stubborn, Suspicious, Shocked, Scared, Shy, Surprised, Troubled, Thrilled, Trusting, Tense, Trapped, Tempted, Uncomfortable, Used, Unwanted, Unhappy, Upset, Vulnerable, Wounded, Worried, Weary, Worthless, Yearning, Zealous.

Rhyming Poems

With rhyming poems, students can experiment with rhyme schemes, the simplest being a couplet:

I doubt that I will ever see
A singer quite like Brittany (Spears)

Or a couple of couplets:

Couplets take so little time
Once you know the way to rhyme

I really can't see for the life of me
What's so hard about poetry

Another rhyme scheme to experiment with is A-B-A-B:

Heart ache is a shattered window that lets in the night

A fever everyone fears to touch

Or going to the prom with your mom, that ain't right

Oh yes, a broken heart can hurt that much

Read your students some examples of rhyming poems
then set them free for some rhyme time of their own.

      I write this to read this to you kids to say
      I'm thankful you're here, kids
            This could be the day
      I reach you and teach you
            to find your own voice

    You've got the chance

You make the choice

There's a world of ideas
      bouncing 'round in your head
and when you write them down, so they can be read
then others might know what you're feeling inside

And they too will write
    and then know the pride
      of sharing a moment
        or speaking their heart

Just a pencil on paper
   That's where it starts

There's a kind of magic
  The way words paint a scene

Do you get the picture?
  Do you understand what I mean?

There's a joy to creating
   To making something new

I hope you'll enjoy writing

   Because it's part of you

Letting the Hurt Out

Students write poems about times they've been emotionally or physically hurt.

Example:

I'm weak in my bones
A heart trapped in hell.
I'm weak in my wings, I need to fly.
If only my tears could wash darkness away

Maybe I'd find enough of Heaven's light,
Maybe I'd find what I'm capable of being.
Maybe I'd find out how beautiful my wings are in sunlight
If only, if only, time wasn't a puzzle.

Higher Power, I know You're waiting for that hour
When I surrender myself to you.
God, I know you're ready to catch me when I break.

And God, I know you know
my wings are beautiful.

If only, If only....

Owees

I knocked a hole in my head skidding out on gravel

    Cut my knee open on a can lid

        Stepped on a rusty nail

            Fell out of an apple tree

                Shot arrows straight up into the air

    Raked a broken drill bit across my thigh

Tore my triceps muscle loose from my elbow doing gymnastics

    Hit the pavement on my motorcycle

        Fell down a cliff and got rope burn

        But other than that, I'm fine

            Just fine.

Need To Wait

Let me tell you it hurts

To tell you how I feel

To say that I love you

And need to wait until

You say something

The silence is killing me

Not knowing what you'll say

Or what might be

This is hurting me

Partner Poems

Students can pick their own partners, names can be paired at random, or the teacher can decide who would work well collaboratively. Each student comes up with (or is given) a starting line and writes it down, then the partners exchange papers, each adding a line or two. They continue exchanging papers until the poem comes to a natural conclusion.

Me: I smiled at a little child today
He: She smiled back and ran away
Me: But as she ran, she turned and waved
He: And as for me, my day was saved

Another example:

Him: My dad's the greatest
She: My dad is never there
Him: My mom is over protective
She: My mom doesn't even care
Him: My uncle had a heart attack
She: Mine got busted selling crack
Him: I want to grow into a great man someday
She: I might just dry up and blow away

Circle Poems

Arrange the students' seats or desks in circles of not more than ten. Ask each student to write a starting line for their circle poem. Then pass the papers to the right with each student adding a new line to the poem. Tell the kids they don't need to rhyme but remind them to keep with the original topic and mood of the poem: this means boys may have to see things from a girl's point of view and vice versa. When the poem returns to the person who wrote the first line, they may choose to edit it, or read it as it is to the class. Note: having students initial the line they write may help prevent them from going off topic with something silly or rude.

Circle poem original:

Gonna die someday
Gonna die very soon
Will someone please help me
Don't be afraid, you'll die sooner or later
Or will you live a long time
Live each day to the fullest
Just enjoy it while you're still alive
Don't worry, be happy
Nothing will go wrong
Life is precious until it ends
And we'll wake up again
I think I believe in reincarnation
Just remember dying isn't bad if you go to heaven

Revision of the preceding Circle Poem Original:

Gonna die someday

Might die soon

    Who can say

        And should I live for years

            Full years

    If nothing should go wrong

        And I live long

        And don't worry

        And don't hurry death

With my last breath

        I might reincarnate

        Or Pearly Gate

But I can't wait to see

    If death will wait for me

In the Stream

This style of poem is a lot like free writing. Challenge the students to experiment with 'stream of consciousness' writing, which is to write down whatever comes into their minds as fast as they can. Of course, they should avoid writing down inappropriate thoughts, but that goes for all assignments. There doesn't have to be "a topic". They can go to an interesting place and concentrate on what's around them, or write in the comfort of their rooms at home, or the classroom. They might try several places and see which one works best for this style of poem.

Example:

The day began dark, first at 2am, then 5:45, sleepless night

I'm alive and writing

inviting you into my pre-dawn morning

of crickets and coffee

quiet sounds

the stream's song

nature rolls over rocks

Country kind of rock and roll

then the first bird utters a word or two

and the sky starts turning toward blue

this is happening to me

is it happening for you?

Stream of consciousness example:

I'm writing these words to show my thoughts

 as they are happening

and who knows where it goes

rhymed

I'm not surprised

It kind of comes naturally
                    To me, see?

It's hard to write as fast as I think
                              I think

I think I think in full sentences
But can't be sure
Until I write them down

And looking around

I see sunshine bouncing off plants

And a mountain out my window

Calling me to go outside…

(I'm gone)

It Talks

The trick to this style of poetry is to give a voice to an inanimate object or a living thing that does not usually speak. Imagine if rocks could talk, cabs could gab, hats could chat, or trees could shoot the breeze. There are just too many things in the world to list here, but I'll suggest a few that might be fun.

If only these things could speak: Your car, an I-pod, a computer, a stop light, a door, a painting, an antique, a gun, the ocean, a mountain, a bike, your clothes, your toothbrush, a road, a bird, an airplane, a bullet, a train, a city, a flower, a dentist's drill, a baseball, a motorcycle helmet, the sun, a carpet, a couch or a television.

For All Those Times

For all those times

     we shared together

You love me,
    don't you?
        Admit it

The Movies
    and Mysteries
        Late nights on the couch

I'm very entertaining
                    You alone
            I can offer you so many things
        If only you were more aware
    You look at me
                    Stare
        But I do all the talking

Would you call me fickle
        just because I can change my image
                        in the blink of an eye?

You   .
        Constantly searching for something you see
                    You need me
        Your sweet TV

Cab Gab

I get people where they're going

And they're always in a rush

Watching my meter

Looking out the window

For the straightest path between point A and B

Cursing the traffic under their breath

Treating the driver like a servant

Not an equal

I've got bumps and scrapes and dings

But I'm alright

It's people who are the strangest things

Sense Poems

Most things we know about our world come to us through our five senses: Taste, Touch, Hearing, Smell, and Sight. Have the students create a poem that utilizes images from at least three of the five senses and that concludes with the students' opinion about the topic they've chosen.

Example:

Looking out across the concert crowd
Their hands raised like a waving field of wheat (sight)
Rock and roll bowls us over like thunder (hearing)
Reverberating against our ribs (touch)
We are sweating pin balls bouncing into each other (smell)
Moved by the music like ripples in a pond (sight)

Another:

My family likes to party
I'm talking steaks sizzling on the grill (scent and sound)
Hugs from all the aunties
Dancing until our feet ache (touch)
And I know it's over when I watch Uncle Al
weavin' his way out the door (sight)
with auntie Fay leading the way
His designated driver
Leaving a trail of her flowery perfume
in every room behind her (scent)

Concrete Poetry

These are words and /or sentences put into shapes that accentuate
the message, making it a visual, as well as auditory, experience.

A
Fir
Tree
Growing
Proud and
Tall, Anchored
Firmly in the Ground
By
Its
Roots

Rap is a trip

Don't be
So square
Just share
Your love
Everything was fine but I knew he was giving me a line every
time he opened his mouth

Today
    I ate two
        éclair
            too many
                So I'm taking
                    The stairs
                        To cut that
                            Fat off
                                At the pass
                                    Before it
                                      Ends up
                                          On my ass

Photo Inspired Poems

Have the students cut out pictures from an old magazine to inspire their poems. If the picture is of a person, they may write about that person or write in the voice of that person telling us what they might say. It may prove helpful to prepare your own stack of interesting pictures to offer students who may have a hard time finding something inspirational.

For example, if the student found a picture of a shark:

Shark Park

Ever take a walk through Shark Park?
Seaweed greenery
On coral kingdom scenery
But beware of visits at dark

The king of that scene
Fast swimming and lean
Has only one thing on his mind

To hunt, always seek
Something easy to eat
Now, isn't it past dinner time?

Night strolls could cost you dear
The kings of Shark Park rule here.

Here's a poem inspired by a bass player in a sequined costume:

Bootsy Collins

I be bad
The rad, glad Dr. Spock of rock

Puttin' down some fine lines
It be rhyme time in this room of tunes

Watch me rip some licks
On my ax, my music stick
My superstar guitar

Yes, it's shine time
As light takes bright flight
Off the little glitter critters
I am entrusted with, encrusted with

So slap and clap those hands
And this music man will rock you
Big time.
So fine.

Muse Music

Play various styles of instrumental music for the students and have them write down what images come to mind when they hear it. Then ask them to pick one of the images and expand on it.

When Words Fail

When words fail, music speaks
Music expresses all the shades of emotion

It's all within the beholder
Nothing can compare with the music within the heart
It's what twinkles with sound

So, you can write with a bleeding pen
Or you can write with an imaginative mind
It doesn't matter
Music conquers all when it's yours
It allows you to stand tall

Rejoice in what you hear
Put spirit into sound
Make it you

Keep it to yourself or be an open book
Willing to be read
When words fail, music speaks

Walk, Man

Summer heat
City street

I boogie bounce by hustle and bustle
    And busses and cusses and traffic jam fusses
(W)Rapped in my I-pod, walkman, discman security
                  Blanket of sound
I cruise this town
    Dancing and strolling
      Rocking and rolling

No, you can't say a word
    Not a one would be heard
    Not a sad city thing

      As I strut like a king
On my musical mountain of sound
    Down town

Song Lyrics are Poetry

Ask your students to bring in the lyrics for some of their favorite songs. It's probably a good idea to remind them that the lyrics must be "appropriate" for the classroom. Each person reads a song as poetry with brief discussion afterwards. The following are some suggestions of lyrics with a message or poetic quality:

John Lennon and Paul McCartney: "She's Leaving Home," "A Day In The Life" "Across The Universe"

Paul Simon: "America" "Old Friends" "Sounds of Silence"

Bob Dylan: "Subterranean Homesick Blues" (the earliest of rap)

Pink Floyd: "Breathe In The Air," "Us and Them," "The Lunatic is on the Grass"

Poems by the Place

Have students choose from the following list, or come up with their own suggestion, and write a poem about a specific place. It can be as close as home or a far off foreign land. It's best if they have first hand knowledge of the place, having been there, but they can use their imaginations if need be:

An attic, a church, a university, a fancy restaurant, a bus, a beach, a farm, the mall, a foreign country, a racetrack, a parade, a plane, a supermarket, a doctor's office, a mountain top, a sailboat, or a cruise ship. Or try a highway, a cemetery, garbage dump, the north pole, a dance, a castle, the principal's office, a submarine, a hot air balloon, the White House, post office, a library, a movie theatre, freeway median, tree house, a closet, goldfish bowl, rest room, toxic waste site, a cemetery, a cave, a desert, the ocean bottom, someone's kitchen, a dentist's office, the South pole, a science lab, a barn, Heaven, the Governor's office, a mansion, an elevator, a palace, a garden, a life raft, a waterfall, the moon, a national park, a ballroom, an island, any large city, traffic court, an oil tanker, a forest, a dungeon, Niagara Falls, a casino, a subway, a skateboard park, around a campfire, a log cabin, a stock exchange, a laundromat, a train station, a stretch-limo, an active volcano, on a submarine, in a cellar, a haunted house, in jail, a nuclear plant, at a hair dresser, a factory, a bar, a drive in movie, a swimming pool, an amusement park, a police station, an operating room, a slaughter house, or a fishing boat.

The Beach

Sand is more
        Than something that sneaks
                Into sneakers
      Is sifted through fingers
     Plastered in castles
It is a massive amount of water
             Showing boulders who's boss
    The futile battle of stone to remain together
It's a highway at low tide
    A moving hill
         Jogging path and moldable bed
      Young minds museum playground
Little chunks of rock, coral and shells
      And other erosion resistant minerals
It's crunchy in oatmeal
      Palatable on peanut butter and jelly
        Not so spicy in soup
But basically, it's all over everything
               at the beach
it's amazing
it's where sea kisses earth
union
shifting alliances and illusions

the softest of stone

Desert

I don't know you
Like you know dust storms and gullies
Dry river beds and rice grass
Geologically fixed rainbows
And rainstorms that never reach the ground
Yes, and the sound no water makes when it isn't helping things
live

Brave, thirsty souls have labored on your stage plateau
Where did they go?
What have you done with them, desert?
Did vultures see and partake?
Is it a mistake to rent from a sandstone tenement?

Coyotes and owls
Star-filled nights when the moon allows
Creatures that can scurry and leap without sound
Hungry eyes are watching
Thirsty days are coming
Think thin and dig in
Into the desert
And sleep with one ear awake
To rain

Rwanda

Screams of the dying

                    travel only so far

Tears for the dead

                    flow only so long

Bodies in rivers

                    wash to the sea

If it's one world

        then this is also killing me

Though I'm insulated by my land of the free

        Security blanket of democracy

Dare I complain about out police state

        when I consider the fate of those

                hacked to pieces in ethnic strife?

Why has life placed me so far from harm?

                Should I sound a global alarm?

                        Or wish upon a shooting star?

I am only one voice

And voices only travel so far.

Bumper Sticker Poetry

The only criteria for Bumper Sticker poems is that they be short enough to fit on a bumper sticker. They can be Haiku, Rhyming, serious or funny. For extra credit, dare them to make their bumper sticker and put it on the family car (for a while, at least)

Visualize Whirl Peas
and a little peace on earth, please

My other poem
Is a sonnet

Honk if you love
Honking

Baby, I'm bored

If you can read this clearly,
You are clearly too close.

All the world's a poem
What are your lines?

Got milk? Eggs?
Let's have breakfast

I love my husband
And I put this on his car
To warn you other ladies to watch out

I brake for
No apparent reason

How's my driving?
Phone 911

War is not the answer
Money is.

Condensed Prose Poems

Have students' free-write on a topic until they have about a page of writing. Then ask them to condense what they've written into ten lines or less. They will need to eliminate many words and phrases and may need to change a sentence or two for it to fit.

Example:

I remember one rainy day at school. I was sitting in Math class staring out the window, watching the water run down the window pane. It looked sort of like tears or maybe that was just my imagination since I was feeling kind of depressed. I had just gotten a "dear John" text message from the girl I thought would always love me. Looking out the window, I noticed there was a crack in the glass near the bottom of the window frame. I thought to myself, well, at least my heart's not the only broken thing around here and that actually made me smile. It's weird how that image helped ease the pain I felt inside.

Rainy
Day
Runs
Down
Window
My Pain
Framed
In Broken Glass
Heart

Free Write Topics

Wind, Rain, Sand, War, Peace, Earth, Friends, Fun, Music, Swimming, Bikes, Toys, Skating, Fear, Love, Sorrow, Joy, Pain, Loss, Holidays, Water, Heaven, Clouds, Computers, Acting, Fighting, Teachers, Parents, Relatives, Travel, Animals, Sports, Players, Television, Movies, Art, Technology, Internet, History, Heroes, Sunsets, Sun, Flowers, Gifts, Jealousy, Anger, Space, Confusion, Exhaustion, Power, Beaches, Hurricanes, Halloween, Christmas, Summer, Sailing, Diving, Hate, Work, Honesty, Wild Animals, Accidents, Being Grounded, Nightmares, Snow, Sight, Churches, Lightning, Blood, Cars, Airplanes, Sickness, Golf, Cartoons, Paddling, Ninjas, Waterfalls, Dirt Bikes, Donuts, Tennis, Boys, Girls, Ghosts, Death, Witches, Faith, Skateboarding, Rock and Roll, Gothic Style, Memories, Stars, Movie Stars, Money, Monsters, Happiness, Sorrow, Jealousy, Cheer leading, Hurts, Babies, Goals, Resiliency, Responsibility, Respect, Resourcefulness, Reading, Bed Time, Rap, Volleyball, Apples, Watermelon, Hiking, Kayaking, Fishing, Camping, Praying, Meditating, Heartbreak, Headaches, Hamsters, Dentists, Clouds, Fire, Eating, Texting, Games, Sports, Embarrassing Moments, Mistakes, The Cosmos, Space Travel, Jobs, America, Cities, Country Living, Boredom, Hope, Grief, Time, Heartbreak, Silliness, Jokes, Pranks, Aging, Relatives, The Future, Thanks, Forgiveness, Global Warming, Pollution, Terrorists, Questions, Driving

Another example of condensing a prose passage into poetry.

I really enjoy a good theological discussion now and then. I will discuss, and cuss, and laugh with anyone from any religion and have a good time doing it. I think many of the principles of most religions are the same. For example, we should treat each other like we like to be treated, be good each other, don't steal or lie. All these values are important. They just need better marketing. God should take out some TV time, hire an advertising company, get some billboards put up with proverbs and catchy phrases. There could be concerts and t-shirts and posters reminding us to live in peace and love one another. That would be good for a change. And if we keep trying to be good, like our hearts tell us do, then evil stuff, all the bad in the world gets the short end of the stick, the back of the bus, or just a real hard time. Yep, just love to rant about religion.

If anyone should ever ask me…
   (and they haven't)
to condense all the holy books
  and make it super simple
    so everyone can understand

I would write just one page
  So it could be on billboards, posters, t-shirts

One page with just two words: Be good

I figure if you're looking for good
  Bad takes a backseat

And what is "good?"

    Let your heart tell you.

Teacher Time

If you would enjoy collaborating with your students in the style of a partner poem, have them hand in a sheet of paper labeled with their name and period, with a starting line (or lines) that sets the mood and direction of poem. Then take their papers home, and in a quiet setting, write the next line (or lines) for each of your student's poems. Then, hand them back the next time you see them so they can add the next line (or lines). It may take a few weeks to complete the entire poem, and it may need some editing before it's considered finished. Not every poem will be a masterpiece, but occasionally, they surprise you. It's a bit of work and time consuming, but if you like to write, it's a fun challenge.

The same?

(two students stand stuck back to back)

She: We're the same as you can see
He: I'm part of her and she's part of me
She: I want to live my life upon the stage
He: Well, I think night clubs are the rage
She: Oh, sure, you'd rather dance and sweat
He: It beats being bloody like Lady Macbeth.

She: Now, let's not argue, there are people here
He: Sorry, I didn't mean to upset you, dear
She: He's always the one to start a fight
He: So that's your game is it? Well, all right!
She: Please hold still. Don't make a fuss.
He: You're the one embarrassing us
She: That's just like you, the first to blame
He: As if you never do the same
She: Ok, you go your way, I'll go mine
(they're still stuck back to back)
He: You see, this happens every time
She: We really should learn to get along
He: You don't say. What are we doing wrong?

Train whistle
A wisp of wind, chilly
Lamplight
A rich man passes a flower seller

A hard day, sir
So many flowers
A shame to see them wilt and die
Kind sir, buy a bit of love

A dollar changed hands

Kindled hope

The rich man caught his train

The flower man
bought the evening bread

He gave the flowers to the doorman

His daughter disliked flowers
Disliked her home
Her father's money
Herself

The flower family
Bent over the bread
Giving thanks

"Your wife's at bridge, sir
And young Freddie called
Said something about needing
More money for school
Will that be all, sir?"

After dinner, he told them tales
Of snow topped mountains
Then it's off to bed

Two martinis
And it's awful to be
Or was it three?

Say your prayers
And sweet dreams kids
I love you so

Another day, another dollar
Poor rich man

First Love

Isn't it funny how close we got?
How I could just be myself around you?
How you became my everything?
My love
My life
My partner in crime
My teddy bear when I need a hug
I thought we were perfect
And meant to be
The way you made me laugh
You made it seem like there were no worries in life and the only
thing that existed was you and me
I regret our fights
Our arguments
Our distrust
Why can't we be just us?

Three Things Poetry

Have the students write several nouns on small scraps of paper, one noun per paper, and place them in a hat or bowl. Then each student picks three nouns at random and must use them in a poem, rhyming or free verse. The same thing can be done with adjectives.

For example: If the nouns were Wish, Earth and Wings…

I wish I was a butterfly

And if you ever ask me "Why?"

I'd say, "I want to flutter by,

To fly on loving wings."

Yes, a Flutter-by in frolic flight

If wish you may,

Then wish you might

For peace on earth

A peace so dear

Now look around.

It's here.

It's here.

If the adjectives were Imaginary, Strange and Little…

Oh, you know…
It may seem strange
The way I can rearrange words
To say something
Or nothing at all
Like scrawl on the wall if you will, and still,
The poet is free
No, I will not be confined by my commentary
Absolutely unrestrained
I'm a run-away train
Not a trained little dog in a circus
Not the least bit bound
I speak for the sake of sound
Bursting around your ear-bones
Like headphones filled with rock and roll
An imaginary stroll on a tightrope of time
And nonsense and rhyme
Just for you

Because that's what poets do.

Deal Me In

Write interesting poetic phrases or combinations of words on playing cards (or three by five cards) and deal the students three to five cards (phrases) to fit into a coherent poem. They can add as many or as few words as possible to have the phrases make sense together. They don't have to use all the cards and can trade them in for others if they're having a hard time with the phrases they've picked.

Yesterday's melodies, Bruised by the rain, Riot Rich, Day break, Summer sun, Dark Skies, Chicken Chatter, Soul Sifting, Thick dreams, Shelter of fear, Invitation, Still standing clouds, Fine, Leaf skeletons, Earth spinning on its axis, Captured and crazy, Space in the race, Miracle of sun, Starving, Breaking rain, mist, mud, plagued by hope, Congratulations, Murmurs echoing, the scent, Constellations, Rusted and bent, Stained, Secret recipes, Not Listening, Make it better, Brilliant courage, Spilling Sky, Be my ears, Never listening, rivers rising, the promise, Churning curses, Moment magic, Hands joined, Celebrations, Out-stretched arms, Memories unloaded, Lost understanding, Ways of waiting, A thousand trumpets, Specks of dust, Breathe, Stone twins, Hushed hate, Loud plastic, Crossed couples, Set a-flying, Fingers crossed, Ginger cookie lives, Planned particulars, My date's parents, Last taste ever, Late with everything, Procrastinating on purpose, Lethal love, Lost laundry, Waste money, Lose money, Doctor's orders, Fortune cookie future, Speeding excuses, Movie title morals, When cartoons go bad, Famous for it, Can you hear me now?, And so are pick-up lines, Nothing in the mail, Aggravating as ever, Questioned by the police, My kind of operation, Mixed up and fixed up, Tattoos for charity, Family misquotes, Best to run, And you should talk, Parachute junky, In the worst way, Break into song, It's always the back of the airplane, They don't sing in prison, Not crying any more, Never a dull moment, So how's that self-esteem?, Day is done, Never keep a secret, Illegal in your head, Desire and frustration, Hope and glory, They've got pills for that now, Lined up and on line, Disgusted by mediocrity, Undeniably drastic, Institutionalized rebellion, Dreams float, Lost everlasting, No time, Lingering on the moment, Lack of leisure, Favorite nonsense, Music of missing,Angles of light, Cornered confessions, Separation, Mountain streaming, Bombs bursting in air, Radical therapy, Cool breeze, Chill pills, Love song, Moments more, Laugh packed, Out of the question, Obvious enjoyment, Excessive force, Twisted judgment, Bone dry, Miserable memoires, The height of your success, The day you're born, Growing down, No joke, Preachin' to the choir, Long story short, The voice that speaks inside, Folk wisdom, Computer compatible, Done in no time, What better way, Reconciliation, Positive vibrations, Borne on a trade wind, Island girl, Look of the land, Don't hide it, Culturally correct, On the shore, Back to you, Good day to cry, Wage peace, Everyone you meet, Spaceship earth child, Heavenly road, Melody in me, Trouble in paradise, Going nowhere, Nothing to lose, Since I found you, Until I get it right, New world, Come back, Close those eyes, Pocket full of blues, Something magical, Star in my car, Like a dream, Walk away, Changing lanes, Diverted destiny, Wrong place wrong time, Such good feelings, Toe tingling happy, Hopeful beginning, Triumphant exit, direct contact, efforts to communicate, Unforeseen events, Crazy day.

For example, if the phrases were 1) Invitation, 2) Out stretched arms, 3) Movie title morals, 4) Nothing in the mail, 5) Stone starved melodies

Consider this rap
Your street level invitation
To keep it real
Don't have to deal with all your
Movie title morals
That bring you down to the street
With outstretched arms
Down to the level of down
Down with it
With all the stone starved melodies
Of the lost poets and rockers who rolled stones
And prayed for moss
Tell it to the boss
Cuz there ain't no money coming
There will be nothing in the mail
And it'll be: "don't call us, we'll call you"
Just take a seat, cuz
You can't keep the beat
You can't take the heat
You're not made for streets like these

If the phrases were: 1) Music of missing, 2) Love song,
3) Reconciliation, 4) Yesterday's melodies, 5) Separation

How can I face today
    When yesterday's melodies
        Are all I seem to remember?

Sweet September love songs
    And October walks in harmony
Your November embrace
    And Christmas kisses

New years' nonsense
    February's fight
The reconciliation of March
    April's shower of tears

May I see you agains
    And June weddings forsaken

July's sad music of missing
    The sweaty blues of summers end

You sing a song of separation to me now
    Such a cool tune

If the phrases were 1) the spilling sky, 2) a thousand trumpets, 3)
angles of light, 4) memories unloaded,
5) lethal love

Just give me the words to say
Then let the poet play
Day break dark skies
Locked in battle, with summer sun,
Over who controls the spilling sky
To celebrate this day

A thousand trumpets of growing thunder
Their murmurs echoing off mountains
Through morning's angles of light
Memories unloaded of rivers rising
So dreams float

Lightning born in hope and glory
Kisses the dessert with love everlasting
Singing stoned starved melodies
Of bombs bursting in air
Amid a chorus of confusion and clouds

Until the incoherent babble of breaking rain
On the pavement, lingering on the moment
Dancing before mountains streaming
The storms lethal love sets poets dreaming
Bone dry despite the flood
I too long to break into song
In the worst way

Poetry of Possibility

Poems of possibility have three stanzas, each with three possible endings for the beginning line of each stanza. They make great postcards: the sender simply checks the ending most befitting his or her mood. These poems need not rhyme and the ending choices can be single words or sentences.

Options

(Check one of the following:)

A day without you is like…
    An eternity
    A day with no sunscreen
    Laughter without lips

I miss your…
    Eyes
    Touch
    Sighs

I just wish you were here…
    So we could talk
    So we could embrace
    So I didn't have to mail this.

Vacation Blues

Here in the Aloha State…
    I've seen the greenest mountains
    I've swam in crystal clear warm waters
    I've sunburned my buns

I honestly…
    Love you
    Miss you
    Am enjoying my space

Be it ever so humble, there's no place like…
    Home
    Hawaii
    You

School Daze

I'm in school and I'm…
    Missing you
    Not missing you
    Having trouble paying attention

Math class is
    So challenging
    So easy
    So unnecessary

Lunch time we should
    Get together
    Share a table
    Smuggle in pizza

<u>Love Ya</u>
    Our romance
        Is moving too fast
        Isn't going anywhere
        Is totally one sided

When I call you up…
        We can talk for hours
        I get voice mail
        You're screening your calls

I want to give you…
        My all
        My love
        Another chance
        Measles

Borrowed, Not Blue

Ask your students to begin a poem with some famous line from literature or a movie or history. You can ask that they finish the poem in a certain style, or a specific rhyme scheme, or a predetermined number of lines or stanzas.

Here are a few phrases for ideas:

I have but one life to give…

To be, or not to be…

It was the best of times' it was the worst of times…

Life, Liberty and the Pursuit of happiness…

Are you talkin' to me?

Frankly, my dear, I don't give a damn.

We'll always have Paris.

There's no place like home.

She's buying a stairway to heaven…

All the world's a stage and we are merely players...

Ask not what your country can do for you…

It is better to have loved and lost…

Give peace a chance…

War: what is it good for?

If at first, you don't succeed…

Early to bed, early to rise…

Just do it…

No news is good news…

Do unto others…

Let them eat cake…

Live free or die…

Live aloha…

Your caring for others is the measure of your greatness…

Cowards die a thousand deaths…

You get fifteen minutes of fame…

A sucker is born every minute…

All you need is love…

(Einstein)A person who never made a mistake never tried something new…

(Stephen Hawking) Intelligence is the ability to adapt to change…

(Dr. Seuss) A person's a person no matter how small…

(Bill Gates) Be nice to nerds. Chances are you'll end up working for one…

Every man dies. Not every man really lives.
William Wallace

Any idiot can face a crisis - it's day to day living that wears you out.
Anton Chekhov

Life must be lived as play.
Plato

A picture is worth a thousand words.
Napoleon Bonaparte

Education is a better safeguard of liberty than a standing army.
Edward Everett

Education is not the filling of a pail, but the lighting of a fire.
William Butler Yeats

A hug is like a boomerang - you get it back right away.
Bil Keane

At the touch of love everyone becomes a poet.
Plato

If we don't end war, war will end us.
H. G. Wells

Every gun that is made, every warship launched, every rocket fired, signifies in the final sense a theft from those who hunger and are not fed, those who are cold and are not clothed.
Dwight D. Eisenhower

A poet is, before anything else, a person who is passionately in love with language.
W. H. Auden

Am I not destroying my enemies when I make friends of them?
Abraham Lincoln

The best thing about the future is that it comes one day at a time.
Abraham Lincoln

Age is an issue of mind over matter. If you don't mind, it doesn't matter.
Mark Twain

I do everything that everybody else does.
Vanna White

The present is a point just passed.
David Russell

I saw the angel in the marble and carved until I set him free.
Michelangelo

A nickel ain't worth a dime anymore.
Yogi Berra

Between two evils, I always pick the one I never tried before.
Mae West

Go to Heaven for the climate, Hell for the company.
Mark Twain

"Am I not destroying my enemies when I make friends of them?

Abraham Lincoln

Am I not
Destroying my enemies
When I make friends of them?
I don't want my enemies
Dead
I was taught to love them
Instead
So Jesus did say
Though war seems reluctant
To pass away
When peace is everything we need
Perhaps it's less hate and more greed
Business decisions and security
Mad over money
And it's all me, me, me

I'd rather follow Lincoln's line
And take all the world
As friends of mine

Someone Else's Poem

Have the student's find interesting pictures of people from sports magazines, fashion magazines, or National Geographic and then compose a poem as if that person were doing the writing.

If the picture was of an angry looking, old, drifter:

God bless America, land of the free
Free to hate each other equally

We'll burn some crosses on you street
Give you ghetto playgrounds, poverty sweet

Discrimination need never show its face
As long as you know to keep in your place

Because we intend to stay on top
Whatever it takes and we won't be stopped.

If the picture was of an Indian:

My tribe, the Cherokee

   Victors of Wounded Knee

Indian Heart
    Tribal Pride
        People of the mountain side

Eagle feathers
    Leather thongs
        Healing chants and ancient songs

You may take this land from me
    Impose your cultural captivity

        But my eagle heart flies forever free

If the picture was a preacher at a pulpit:

On Fire

The world is on fire

And the heat abounds

Surrounds everything

But the living is cool

In the shadow of the cross

Of one put down

Small town

Carpenter King

If the picture was of a person in a strong wind:

Sometimes you have to blow people away
                    Just to bring them together

A whirl wind of weather
                That can cause heartache and pain

            A hurricane

Relief if it missed you   hurt if it kissed you

            Life takes a big time out and everything
                            stops

                    they close up the shops

                gather the family near
                        huddle in fear
                under that sky so grey
                        in a most unusual way

yes, I was scared

and yes, I was spared

In a Style

Challenge the kids to write a poem in a certain style such as: Movie clichés, Scary Story, Valley-speak, Shakespearian, Revival meeting, Talk show, Hip hop jargon, Stone age cave dweller, Auctioneer, Game Show MC, Scholar, Drill Sergeant, or Comedian

Bard Style:

All the world's a poem, a stage
And this is merely words
That wonder, fuss and fret
            mere moments upon this page
and then are read
            silently signifying nothing.
A tale told to an idiot
        full of Shakespearian fury
All is vanity
Lost in poetry
        sweet insanity of sound and who knows
                where this might lead…
Indeed,
        in jest,
            the rest is yet to come
                    from some future bard in time

> Hard rhymes
> Is soft seclusion
> The illusion
> Of some grad design

That orescapes these lines

Fine.

In the style of a student protest leader:

If ever the government
        Federal   State
            Judicial

Authorities that be
        Try to tell me
            I cannot be free
                As I see fit
    Then that's it

I will gladly return all the little plastic cards
                papers and passwords
            numbers and networks
all ID that dares

define me
and they can come find me in the hills
    waking to the birds

        far away from the words: do dis and dat

        When one lives free
            there seems no better way to be.

In the style of a confused teenager:

Every thought has its contradiction
As if I must be
    A system of checks and balances
Another example of the failure of democracy
Every dream has its fear
And every question
    Has the habit of leading me
        To a single pile of "I don't knows"
I sit in the unknown
    Back against some merciless wall
        Awaiting discovery
        Personal recovery
From the prominent contradictions I've created
"Why did I do that?"

"Why am I here?"
        "Who runs this show?"
And the silent reply is always
        "I don't know."

In the style of greedy corporate CEO's:

Multi-nationals
    Big men business
        Pushing and shoving and loving
                Their money
    Maintaining poverty
    Pretending integrity
    Protecting their assets and asses
        Third world manipulation
        Freedom's capitulation
            "Please, Uncle Sam,
                beat on that bad man
                    who dares nationalize me.
    Land of the Free
                        crush him
                        consume him

to make room for me
and my money bag biggy bank
For mine is the money
And power
And glory
Without end,
though no one understands

I've got the whole world in my hands
And I want more…

In the style of a third world terrorist:

Little boy Amerikan
Born and bred
Flag colors of pure white
True blue

                         And blood red

Be rich and be proud

                              Your Uncle Sam said

Major in money

                    Then maybe you'll wed

It's a dog eat dog world

                         But your family gets fed

Visions of Cadilacs dance in your head

And maybe they'll bury you in one

                         When you're dead

Repetition Poem

Have your students create poems that have a line or phrase that repeats occasionally throughout the poem. It should be a strong sentence that emphasizes an important message of the poem.

You're quick to laugh
And I like that
You cheer me up
Give of your time
Encourage me to do my best
And I like that
We can enjoy each other's company
Even when it seems there's nothing to do
Being together is all that matters to us
And I like that
And every now and then
You tell me how important our friendship is
And I like that best of all.

See God

See
God
See
God doesn't just sit in His chair
See

So
God
See
God could be
        Should be
                Just might be here, now
See

So
Now
See
God is trying
 Has been trying
        Will keep on trying to give us new sight
New light, see?

So
Now
You See
God doesn't just sit in his chair.

Forget Love

You can pray and preach
                Bow and chant
                        Meditate and contemplate
            But don't forget love
You can climb mountains
        And sit surrounded by bird song breezes
            But please, don't walk away from love
You can talk to your friends
        e-mail everyone you know   bounce ideas off
        satellites in space
        but don't forget to mention love wins
You can be rich and famous
                Envied and pampered
                        Able to buy a slice of paradise
But my advice is to spend some time
                Looking for the loving thing

            Then sing, dance, sculpt, write
        and try to create more love
wherever you go
        however much you can
            no matter what you do
                don't forget to love.

Too Much

It's ok to drink
    But don't drink too much
        Or you may be seen as an alcoholic
          Or lose your job
            Crash your car
              Hit rock bottom
It's ok to think
    But don't think too much
        Spend all your time worrying
Recycling the same hatreds and fears

It's ok to care
    But don't care too much
        Lest you lose yourself in others
    Spending so much time feeding their needs
That you're starving

It's ok to dream
    But don't dream too much
        Become lost in fantasy
          Moments of imagining
            Never touching reality
And it's ok to love
    Because you can't love too much
        And if you do, no one will mind.

Nonsense

Students might find it fun to be set free from the need to make sense. They can just play. Play with language. Play with sound. Experiment with rhyme and phrasing. Make up words or put words together in strange ways.   Reminiscent of E.E. Cummings.

Stumble Upon Me

If someday

As you are searching

Through the depths of nothing

With width of eternity

The outside of in

If by chance to stumble

Upon me

Anywhere

Send me home

I'm lonely

Simple ditty
Lady pretty
Skip a dip a doorknob
Silly girly
Mother of pearly
Ocean notion heart-throb
Hold me cozy
Blushes rosey
Thorny love stories gone glad
And had you gone…

Tears.

No Sense

How many are

    This

Or   those that are here
       ?

It 'tis and 'twas and 'tweren't no more

A snicker in your ear

Yes, snarl your best

        For what is worst?

          So high that all may see

And be it now
        Or when or then
Or never it will

      be.

Go Together Poems

These poems are a romantic tribute to someone real or imaginary. The following guidelines will help, but students don't have to use them all and they can be put in any order.

List things that fit together

(ex: pieces of a puzzle)

List foods that go together

(ex: peanut butter and jelly)

List people you associate together

(Ex: Batman and Robin)

List things you associate together

(ex: moonlight and romance)

Also consider: things that are close, essential, or connected; things that need each other or that are found together in nature.

End with one big reason why the two of you should be together

(ex: because without you my dreams would be broken like chunks of surf boards washing up on the rocks)

Together

We are close
As the ABC's
Close as can be
Like the 123's
We connect
Like electric current
Or magnets
We fit
Like a favorite pair of jeans
We need each other
Like a pencil needs paper
Or shoelaces need shoes
We communicate
Like actors and directors
Or CIA code specialists
My life without you would be
An empty bowl of cornflakes
Filling with tears
Because we go together like
Fish and poi
Sunshine and swimming pools
Pizza and Pepsi
Dreams and rest
You're the best

Hat on Head

We should go together,
Because we go together like birds of a feather,
Peanut butter and jelly,
Bread and butter,
Milk and cookies,
We join together like puzzle pieces,
Nuts and bolts,
Links in a chain,
We work together like
Ben and jerry,
Dave and busters,
Starbucks and jamba juice,
We fit together,
Like a ring on my finger,
A hand in glove,
Or hat on head,
We make a good team,
Like Shaq and Kobe,
Batman and Robin,
Sonny and Cher
Tom and Jerry,
Sponge Bob and Patrick,
Daffy and Bugs,
We should go together forever,
You don't want to do it alone.

Cookies and Cream

We should go together
  Because we go together like
Fries and ketchup
Milk and cereal
Cookies and cream
Cream and sugar
Ice cream and root beer

We fit together like
Computers and keyboards
Pencil and paper
Thread and needle
Cars and wheels
The moon and stars

We make a good team like….
Zack and Cody
Brad and Angelina
The Ying Yang twins
Pharrel and Snoop Dog

We fit together like….
Chili and rice
Salt and pepper
Popcorn and butter
Strawberries and whip cream

We should go together because we belong together.

Poems for your family

This is more a specific topic than it is a style of poetry. This could be an opportunity to practice several styles. Have the students pick three different relatives and three different styles of poem. They could read the one they feel came out best to the class. (If they're shy, I schedule "private readings for the teacher" after school.)

Baby's Day

Hey little one, how was your day?
Too young to crawl, to draw, to play.
What did you do girl, give me the scoop?
"Same as yesterday, eat, sleep and poop."

Just a few weeks old and cute as a button.
Don't tell me you just lazed around
Not doin' nothing.
Did you learn new things?
Make memories to keep?
"Hard to say when you just
poop, eat and sleep."

Well, you just keep on growing
You've got all the time in the world
We love just to watch you and hold you

You're such a good girl
It's a wonderful world
With so many nice people to meet
But for now little girl
You just poop, sleep and eat.

Gee, Grandfather G.

I wonder
Did it bother you
that you never knew me
That you weren't around to see
what your genes contributed
What I was going to be
Your grandchild turned man child

You must have had blue eyes
Grandma said you also had eyes for the ladies
Was the womanizing worth it?
Does some of that sex drive surge through me?
Will it affect my marriage to be?
Will it take my grandchildren from me?

I cannot meet you now
When the Social Security checks stopped coming
Grandma said, "He must be gone and good riddance."
But gee, Grandfather G.
I would have liked you
to know me.

Questions Only Poems

For Question Poems, students don't worry about rhythm or rhyme, but rather concentrate on asking questions that are important to them. They can try to supply answers or be content with just finding meaningful questions.

Example:

Were we created or have we evolved?

Has there ever been a time of real peace on the planet?

Why doesn't God seem to be more personally involved in life on earth?

Are there other creatures with tears?

What's beyond the furthest star?

Who will want to marry me?

How does it all end?

Seven Whys, a What and a How

Why do people who loved each other enough to have children get divorced?

What happens after we die?

Why is it so hard to be honest with one another?

Why does our country have money for war but not enough to feed the poor?

Why are the stars so far away and will we ever travel there?

Why do hurricanes happen?

Why are there clouds?

How did they build those pyramids?

Why does love feel so good and then hurt?

Poems Built Around a Question

Have the students ask themselves: "What is it I wonder about?" or "What puzzles me about this crazy world of ours?" Then have them try to come up with their own answers. These poems don't need to rhyme. The criterion is staying with the problem/solution framework.

Ending Hunger

Why are there millions of people starving?

Don't some countries have trouble with obesity?

Isn't there enough for all?

Do we lack the compassion to share?

Is food a political weapon?

Or do we simply procreate too well?

<u>Prophets of War and War Profits</u>

Why is there war?

Is it history's way
of keeping the population down?

Is it all about age old hatreds?

Is it because people are different
colors or religions?

Or is it just about making some rich people
all the more richer?

And if that's the case,
How can we learn to profit from peace?

Life 101

Ask your students to write a free verse poem about some of the important things they've learned about life so far. I recommend you write one yourself first and read it to them along with other examples to set the tone and help give them an idea what you're looking for.

Forty

Old enough to know better
Still too young to care
Having lost some of my idealism
Still holding onto my hair
Glad for all I've learned
Still yearning to know more
Happy to have loved
And know what love is for
Just a little bit creaky
I can feel some muscles ache
But not afraid to exercise
Considering what's at stake
A little bit skeptical

Still a little overweight
A legend in my own mind
Fame and fortune, fickle fate
Thankful to be living
For my wife, the kids and friends
If this birthday brings me middle age
I want another forty before it ends.

Check This Out

Everything
        And everyone is a piece of stardust
                So shine

And human beings are blessed
            Because we can create nice things
(and sometimes not so nice things)

I suggest we do our best
        to create only nice things
and be nice to one another
        love each other
                as much as we love ourselves
                        (which is a lot)

Love is one the most beautiful things we can create

Live in peace with yourself
          And others
                    And all the world
Reflect good and never hate

Be a light in dark places
          The fastest, brightest, prettiest thing is light
                    You too are light, alright?
                              So shine
          All the time
          Until the day you die and fly as light
                    (Heaven knows where)

Avoid negativity in thought, speech and action

Hate hurts you
          Makes you feel bad

Think the best
          And hope the most

Fill your mind with love, joy, and awareness

Love your life and live your life with love

Treat people like you like to be treated

Be giving and don't steal

Don't live your life in fear

     Afraid of what people might think

Life is full of polarity

   The Yin Yang, good/bad, high/low, dark/light, you know

    But look for the unity

     Consider the wholeness of life

We are all different and yet, we are all one

This world isn't heading to an end

It's heading to a start and it starts with you

   And all you can be

As the loving creator created you to be

The world isn't ending, it's beginning with you.

New Word Poems

Read Lewis Carol's "Jaberwocky" to the class and discuss what the made up words may mean. Then show them some of the following examples and ask them to create poems with their own made up words. These poems should be easy to rhyme since they can make the words sound the same.

Have you seen my snitzle?
I lost it at the whoop dee doo
It's a plucky bit of fitzle
And you can have some too!
Yes, there's nothing like a snitzle
When the day turns cold or gray
Though folks may flap their goopers
Who cares what people say?
Snitzles for the masses
At dawn of doople time
Come and find my glasses
And we'll go look for mine

Fantasy

Challenge your students to use their imagination to create a poem about a place or creature that does not exist in the real world; where things are quite different from the real world.

Example:

Someone Must Take a Stand

Once upon a flip flop
There lived a Vorpal Snit
Who rode a fransome gopler
And spoke with words of glit
But a fierce and flying krunster
Brought terror to the land
And all the folks of Frickfrack said,
"Someone must take a stand!"
"Fear not, you pluffer gunkles,"
Said the fearless Vorpal Snit.
"I shall face that flying krunster
And I'll glip it where it flits."
'Twas a fierce and noscious battle
With fire and screams and slopter

But victory came at last
To the Vorpal Snit atop his fransome gopler
And now, throughout the land
Glimsome songs are heard
"All hail the Vorpal Snit
Who saved us by his bravery and glerd."

Yesterday, Today and Tomorrow

This three part poem is concerned with a person's past, his or
her present situation and his or her hopes for the future.

Yesterday I was the rain-like tears of loss
       And loneliness

Today I am the sun, shining love into joy
       To warm all hurt hearts

Tomorrow I will be the wind to cool your fevered fears
       and ease the ache
            of aging years

Yesterday I was old news

Soon to be forgotten scandals
Celebrity separations
Today I am the latest fatalities

Gene therapy breakthroughs
And box office billions

Tomorrow I will take rich folks to the edge of space
Power my car with a fuel cell
And welcome many more babies
to an ever more crowded world

Yesterday I was so glad to be a kid
Determined not to get a moment older
I knew I had it good

Today I have reached respectability
Accept responsibility
And put aside childish things

Tomorrow I'm hoping for wisdom
A slowed down peace of mind
Maintaining my faculties
Still in touch with the child in me

Proverbs and Poetry

This may not seem to be poetry but it's a lot of fun so bear with me if I include this. The trick is to be funny, not finish the phrase with the correct answer. You can discuss with the students what the correct ending for each proverb is, but you don't have to. You can have the students pick one of their proverb ideas and expand it as a poem in itself. The important thing is to have fun. Education should be fun whenever possible.

Examples of Proverbs

The early bird catches…(the worm) no moss

Early to bed, early to rise, makes you…(healthy, wealthy and wise) tired and grumpy and early.

A penny for your…(thoughts) pocket

Don't put all your eggs in one…(basket) Easter Bunny

Don't count your chickens before…(they hatch) breakfast

His bark is worse than …(his bite) his breath

Beggars can't be…(choosers) bankers

When the cat's away, the mice will…(play) party

Two heads are… (better than one) bound to argue

You're barking up the wrong…(tree) metaphor

The hand that rocks the cradle… (rules the world) changes the diapers.

A bird in the hand is worth two… (in the bush) fifty, at least.

There is no honor among…(thieves) politicians

Many hands make light…(work) bulbs

As easy as falling off …(a log) the wagon

Don't put the cart before the…(horse) groceries

Haste makes…(waste) stress

The straw that broke the camel's…(back) will to live

You can't teach an old dog…(new tricks) algebra

Don't let the cat out of…(the bag) the kitchen

That's a horse of a different…(color) persuasion

In the nick of…(time) knock

Like a bull in…(a china shop) BVD's

He's got a chip on his…(shoulder) chaps

Don't burn the candle at…(both ends) bedtime

Take it with a grain of…(salt) rice

Beating around the…(bush) head

I'll keep by fingers…(crossed) clean

I got it straight from the horses…(mouth) association

Keep it under your…(hat) umbrella

Fast as greased…(lightning) goose

Don't get left holding the…(bag) laundry

Out of the frying pan and into (the fire) rehab

You're the apple of my…(eye) lunch

Through thick and…(thin) thicker

Keep the ball…(rolling) on your side

It was a wild goose…(chase) gizzard

Wet behind the… (ears) shower curtain

By hook or…(crook) hangnail

A wolf in sheep's…(clothing) sleep

Beggars Need Love Too

The early bird catches the bus.

    Early to bed, early to rise, makes you healthy,

        wealthy and tired.

A penny for your child support.

    Don't put all your eggs in your mouth.

        Don't count your chickens before they die.

His bark is worse than his breath.

    Two heads are better than five crack heads.

        Beggars can't get girlfriends.

When the cat's away, the mice will play monopoly.

The Wrong Cat

You're barking up the wrong cat.

Many hands make a mess.

That's as easy as falling off a cow.

A bird in the hand is worth a dollar fifty.

Don't put the cart before the bus.

Don't let the cat out of the bath.

Two heads are better than tails.

Beggars can't be fun.

Don't put all your eggs in one chicken.

A Penny For Your Nickel

Early to bed, early to rise,

    makes you healthy, wealthy and stubborn.

Don't put all your eggs in one pair of pants.

    His bark is worse than his butt.

        The early bird catches a ride.

Early to bed and early to rise

makes you healthy, wealthy, and surprised.

    A penny for your nickel.

        Beggars can be losers.

    You're barking up the wrong fish.

The early bird catches the nerd.

    But don't put all your eggs in one pocket.

How To Write A Love Poem

Students may choose some or all of the following suggestions to create their love poems:

Begin by finishing the phrase "Love is…" as many ways as you can.

Write about how it makes you feel: the hurt or the happiness.

Write about what you imagine it will be like.

Write about romantic places.

Write about things that symbolize love.

Write about the responsibilities love brings.

Write about how to make love last.

Compare love to other things using similes. (love is like the air we breathe, we need it to survive)

Try to think of one word to describe it all.

End with a statement about what kind of love you want.

<u>Example:</u>

Love is lonely
Without you
Love is easy
When I look in your eyes
Love is amazing
To know you care

I hurt when you hurt
Dream the same dreams
Wake with you on my mind
Smile with every memory

We could go to college together
Cramming for tests in a tangled mess
Lost in each other's arms

We could be married at sea
With dolphins as ring bearers
And sea gulls for singing

We can have breakfast in Paris
Lunch by the Pyramids
Dinner in deepest, darkest Africa

I will shower you in roses
You can cover me in candy kisses

I will sit by your side if you're sick
You can rub my sore shoulders when work is hard

We will each day discover love anew
And I will strive to be the better part of you

You are bird song in my morning
I'll be the butter on your toast

It will be all togetherlyness
In our love's nest

Joyous
Just to be near you is enough
With hugs and kisses when times are rough

You Can Fall

One wish keeps you trying
Looking for that silver lining
You can fall a thousand times
Feeling like you've lost your mind
But love will find a way

We can all learn to love again
Trust again
Our hearts will mend
Tears will dry
We will survive

It only takes a moment to change your life
Only a dream to keep you wondering
Only a little love to light your way

Speak Of Love

Love is the happiest of all emotions

It makes you feel amazing inside

Love sounds like angels playing their majestic harps

With harmonies beautiful and soothing for the soul

Our hearts strive to beat to those heavenly rhythms

To speak of love, To dream it

To hold it in our hands

A brief, gentle moment

To feel spectacular love

The fire, the light, the warmth

That can live in us all

Dig deep to find it

Make it your mission to uncover it

And every day is made worth living

By love, Wonderful love

By the Numbers

Ask your students to create a poem that deals with numbers in some way. It can include numbers, be about numbers, have numbered lines or words or syllables. It's OK to show them a few examples, but give them the opportunity to surprise you.

When Less is More

8   Love is all I have to give you

7   Love is all I have to give

5   Love is all I have

3   Love is all

2   Love is

1   You

You're the (1) for me
And I love you (2)
I will be there (4) you
Bring you warm soup on (6) days
Yes, I think of you off-10
24-7

All Together Now

Love Is: A collaborative Valentines poem project for the whole class:

Have the students finish the phrase, "Love is…" as many different ways as they can in a ten-minute period.

Have them type their answers in one computer file that can then be edited by the teacher or the students themselves.

You'd want to take out lines that are repetitious or too similar.

You may want to group lines that seem to be about the same aspect of love such as romance, dating, love of family, etc.

Example of a compilation of student ideas on what love is about:

Love Is…

Love is butterflies in your stomach
Someone who cares and comforts you
Love gives you hugs when you're down
Love is someone special saying "good morning"
Love is the sun's shining rays
on a freezing morning
Love is feeling refreshed and ready for the world
But can be feeling hurt and not knowing what to do
Love is holding hands in the park
Seeing that person's face
It's laughter between friends
Love is the windy breeze through a hot day
or sharing an ice cream cone
It's waiting for the his or her call, anxiously
Love is a special feeling
Love lives in our hearts
Love is hugs and kisses
Happiness
Love is caring for each other
Its chocolate, roses and flowers
Love is hard to explain
Love is hope
and trust
Love is looking into that person's eyes
knowing they're the one for you
Love is having respect for each other

Love is blind
Love is liking the person for who they are
Something that will never go away
It's like soaring through clouds at sunset
Love is knowing
that person will never let you go
A promise to each other
Love is great
Love is caring
Love is cool
Love is exciting
Love is kissing
It's complicated
Hard
Heartless
Stupid
Love is warm
Love is belief
Love is faithful
Love is sweet
Sad
Scary
Love is waiting five more minutes
for the bathroom
It's moon-lit dinners
A midnight walk on the beach
Caring no matter what race, age,
or religion you are
Its trust and respect
World peace
Beautiful, sweet music
Pride and joy for one's country
Flowers after a fight

Love is letting others have
their fifteen minutes of fame
It's caressing a new born baby
Sharing prosperity
Love is writing a sweet poem for your honey
The giggles that he gives you
when you're feeling down
Love is his t-shirts that you wear
whenever you miss him
Late night walks on the beach watching the stars
Love is his beautiful brown eyes
The cuddles he gives you
just to keep you safe and warm
Love is the look on his face
when he tells you how much he loves you
Love is flowers in vases
The confusing looks he gives you
that drives you crazy
Waiting all night for his phone calls
Love is the notes that he writes you
That makes your heart melt into pieces
Love is sushi on the beach watching the sunset
Kissing under the moon
Gifts that he buys you
even when it's not your birthday
Love is the messages on your phone
saying how much he loves you
Knowing that you're loved
Ice cream and cakes while watching a movie
Love knows that you can be yourself
around him without feeling uncomfortable
Love is the feeling in your heart that takes your breath away
whenever he is around
Love is a rollercoaster ride
Always smiling

Spending the whole day at school together
Walking together holding hands
Always thinking and dreaming of him
Crying about him when you break up with him
Always loving him no matter what happens
Love is Valentines Day
Doing something kind for someone
other than yourself
Chocolate
Hugs
Love is supposed to last forever
When you're sad, your boyfriend or girlfriend cheers you up
Love is not love at first sight
Love takes time and grows
Love is the cure
Without love, you would be nothing
Love will never leave you with heartache
It will never deceive you
Real love does not care what you look like
or how you act
It's a feeling of joy in your heart
Sharing what's inside you with others
Something that can't be taken out of you
Mysterious
Something that can happen in an instant
Love is everywhere
Sitting on a cliff and watching the sunset
Dancing under the moon
A need
An ingredient to your health
It's not always fair
It can be the missing part of a person
Something that needs to be found in everyone
A bond between two people
Love is priceless

It's the best gift to give anyone
It's extraordinary
Sweet
Going on dates
Exploring the world
Holding hands in the movies
It's the taste of cherry pie
The morning sky
Hope
Faith
Kindness
Being thankful
Love is difficult
Going out of your way for someone
Love is just staring at each other
Love is being sorry
for all the things I say or do wrong
Holding each other
Giving her your jacket to keep warm
Making a difference
Love is staying on the phone
Even when no one's talking
Respecting the other person's choices

May you find love

What Love Is

Everything you could wish for
The best feeling in the world
Pure joy
Love is beautiful
Powerful
Perfect
Patient
Healing
Accepting
Unconditional

It's the most wonderful thing
Love is for everyone,
forever
Love is whatever you want it to be

Happy
Laughing
Beautiful
Romantic

Love is a four letter word
A stormy day
A figment of the imagination
Blind

It can be hurtful
Depressing
Brutal
Messed up
Horrible
Irritating
Aggravating
It's sad
Stupid
Hurtful
Scary

It's a stress causer
A bluff
A fake
Junk
Weird

Love is expressed in different ways
It's everywhere
It's holding hands together
Watching the sunset together
Kissing each other
Like heaven
Compassionate

Love is trusting someone
Full of happiness and heartache for everyone
Sometimes making each other cry
But love is always worth it

Love is an emotion
Fragile
Confusing
Unstable
Changing
Temporary
Something that can vanish
Ironic
Hard to keep
Something some people can't find
Awkward
Crazy
Complicated

An unbeatable feeling
A strong word
Risky
Wonderful
Free
Astonishing at times
Worth more than hate
Never boastful nor conceited
A serious commitment
Two souls connecting together
Genuine
Devotion
Exciting
A promise
A challenge
Sacrifice
Irreplaceable

Love is more than a crush
It's giving someone your heart
Having faith in one another
Listening to each other
It's time spent with that special person
who is everything to you
So important
So awesome
Thinking about them
Late night calls
Talking
Respecting your love
Writing to each other
Being held when tears fall

Love can change people

It can happen to anyone

Write a Rap

I was born in the age of rock and roll but I can appreciate rap for what it brings to poetry. There have been some outstanding experiments in rhythm and assonance and rhyme because of rap. If it keeps poetry alive on the street, I'm all for it. I don't really know how to teach kids to write it since I figure they've got more experience with it than I do. It just seems to use lots of rhymes in short succession while expressing the human condition: be it love, frustration, poverty, or an egotistical effort to be the master of the mike.

The Un-rap

The name is Joe Cool
And I hate to rap

I think that city slicker stuff just sounds so whack
They take their master ghetto blaster and their microphone
And they dance the boogy woogy while textin' on the phone

They don't sing it
They wing it and hey, that bothers me
The way they mutilate the language and call it poetry

Well if you love rap I feel sorry for your soul
'Cuz rap is for them that can't rock and roll

The Following are Titles for some Rap style poems:

Living In Paradise

When I Rule the World

Can't Nobody Tell Me Nothin'

Whole Lotta Love

Why the Ladies/Guys Love Me

We Rule the Schools

I'm A Lover, Not A Fighter

Looking For More

Fame For The Lame

Give It Time

You're Not Gonna Get Me Down

If That's The Way It Is

The Best I Can

Love Sets You Free

What's Up, Dog?

Slippin' Back

Gotta Be Me

Proud To Be Free

East Side Man/Gal

When I'm Free

I'm So Cool It Hurts

Chill Out, Shout Out

Tuning Things Around

Hit With A Hurt

Man On The Move

Standin' Up To You

Pick UpThe Pieces

I'm Outta Here

Memory Music

Lost in Trouble

Take You There

Lie To Me

City Streets

Never, never ever

Sidewalk Fantasy

Sailor Boy

So Fine

Need Some Rain

Miss Me Man

Play The Game

Changin' It

Raining All Over

It Ain't Easy

I Need More

Leave It Alone

Travel Time

Uptown Life

Punk's Life

Hungry Tonight

Dressed to the Nines

Sweatin' Summer

Cruisin'

When It's All Over

Come On Over

I Got Time

Got Me Dowh

Down With That

Do It Yourself

Don't Push It

Who Says?

Life's Changes: "Daddy Don't"

He witnessed a horrible death
Ended up hooked on meth
Had unsafe sex
Now he's tied to a single mother
With no alibi
With no money
Just tears in the baby's eye
If you start to cry it's OK
Mom's workin' three jobs
Just to make her way
It may be hard to hear but this is reality
No fairy tales
It's actuality
Li'l boy growing up asking, "Where's Daddy?"
Momma, how you going to lie your way out of this one
and keep him happy?
Find out what's been happening and start to cry
Knowing that his life is messed up cuz daddy left him to get high
So he sits back and sighs
Lets a tear drop down his eye
No more partying on the sly
Has to be the man of the house
This is what it's all about
Think about the consequence
Always listen to your conscience
Drop out of high school to support the family
This is one fairy tale never lived out happily
Where's your daddy?
Turn around. Look at the name on the tombstone in the ground
Rest in peace
Silence rather than sound
Life is a game uncontrolled
Look out for your soul

Free Stylin'

I can rearrange words, strange birds flying through blue sky and only I know why, the reasons for what I do or why the sky's blue or the dirt is brown.

A sound clown who wears a frown lookin' down at the ground, mad at the world for what he has become, puttin' make-up on for an audience to watch him act dumb, juggling pins.

Forgive our sins, for we're tempted like any other, a mother or a brother, sister son or daughter, we're all the same, playin' the same game with different names, lookin' for fame but that's not what we need, this advice you need to heed, every day we go the same way not knowing what to say and we may but the Lord's the only way.

And hey, every night as I go to bed my face turns red there's ringing in my head from the yelling of my sisters giving me blisters in my ears and I fear I won't be able to sleep and I have to count sheep so I can get some rest.

And yet when I close my eyes and the rest of the world dies, I'm awakened again and the night has come to an end and I must get up and get ready and I'm unsteady as I move not fully awake my legs shake with exhaustion. I feel like I'm lost and lonely but I'm only in the hall, ready to fall, just forget it all: but I can't cuz I gotta go to school, gotta start anew and now I'm ready, hey crew...are you?

Chinkle Chankle

Well, you talk about income
I'd sure like some
A little dough don't you know and I could get down
but there's just not enough green stuff around.
and that's money

I've got a coupon, can I win that prize
At your bargain basement computer compromise?
You got a sale I can save on everything I see
Just like the garbage on my home TV.
You know I wanna buy it all though it's working me dead
I'm a TV kid with a TV head
Yes, I sit up with my set in the middle of the night
Just to fall asleep by the TV light
Then I wake up in the morning to the news each day
And they say everything's a mess and it'll never go away
And I get deeper in debt brother every day

Chinkle chankle, I'd like a whole bank full
I'd be so thankful, yea, for some money

Raisin' my rent, my money's spent
I hear there's war in the government
I'm hopin' for a settlement

I don't need napalm, A-bombs or H-bombs
Battleships at sea or missiles over me

I'm in love with my life and I'm happy just to live
And if I had money, no, I wouldn't give it
to blowin' things up
or tearin' things down
Listen children, what's that sound?
Everybody gotta stop what's goin' down
with your money, cuz it's your money

We've got to tell those boys
That the price of their toys is too high to pay
And everyone, everywhere, everyday needs money

There's sure a lot of rich people I know
Got more than they need but they'd never let it go
Now, why don't they share some
It's only fair to spare some money for the people
We're talkin' board and bread
Besides, you can't take it with you
brother when your dead

It's only money.

A Broken Heart

You could also call this style of poem, "Really Sad Things" but for the romantics in the crowd, we're writing about heartbreak. Even if the kids haven't been in love yet, they know that heartbreak is sad and painful and if they can come up with five to ten painfully sad moments, they've satisfied the criteria for this type of poem.

Example:

A Broken Heart

A broken heart is like a night with no stars

    Or going to the prom with your mom

It's a shattered window that lets in the cold

    A world with no smiles or children's laughter

The sound of old love songs
    played through blown out speakers

The taste of spoiled milk with burnt toast

It's a guitar with no strings, no song to play

A stillborn kitten

The tears of a teen lost

    on homeless streets in a city at night

A fever everyone fears to touch

Oh yes, a broken heart can hurt that much

A Broken Heart

A broken heart is like sitting too long
    on a cold cement seat

    It's like bowling pins that won't reset

    Sobs hidden in pillow stuffing

It's like remembering the correct answer for a test
    after you already turned it in

    Like lickin' an ashtray

    Farm fields reeking of radiation

A bad case of the "what's to become of me?" blues

    Feeling so out of touch

    Oh yes, a broken heart can hurt that much

Broken

Broken bottles
Broken dreams

Scattered glass
Tattered seams

Lost and lonely
No one cares

Everyone's out there
Feel their stares

Should be easy
Just takes time

I'm broken now
But I'll be fine

Don't open old wounds
Let things heal

You can't say you've been there
If you don't know how I feel

Writing "Ation" Poems:

Students are to use several of the following words to create a poem with a rap/rhyming style: (this is a good opportunity to grab a dictionary and learn the meaning of some new words)

Temptation, relaxation, sophistication, taxation, representation, presentation, constipation, publication, quotation, confirmation, situation, starvation, sensation, conversation, stimulation, creation, transformation, fascination, admiration, dedication, recommendation, irritation, hospitalization, equations, memorization, nation, information, clarification, capitalization, punctuation, administration, isolation, identification, obligations, contemplation, inspiration, limitations, appreciation, imagination, emancipation, aggravation, destination, consideration, declaration, dedication, insinuation, complication, computation, personification, infatuation, maturation, accusation, suffocation, carnation, donation, citation, damnation, vibration, elation, graduation, location, probation, salvation, sedation, vocation, celebration, compensation, confiscation, delegation, desolation, imitation, legislation, moderation, observation, occupation, operation, pollination, navigation, population, termination, vindication, variation, accumulation, assassination, certification, collaboration, communication, continuation, determination, discoloration, discrimination, equalization, impersonation, recommendation, evaluation, decoration, specialization, standardization, westernization, education, application, organization, reservation, fixation, innovation, meditation, compensation, Radiation, detoxification, disqualification, insubordination, interpretation, illumination, industrialization, dislocation, miniaturization, characterization, telecommunication, civilization, inflammation, rehabilitation, corporation, association, adaptation, annexation, animation, aviation, congregation, consolation, constellation, dehydration, deportation, devastation, fabrication, hesitation, infestation, installation, medication, perspiration, pollination, proclamation, demonstration, implication, conservation, sanitation, laceration, justification, estimations, desolation, separation, elimination, segregation, affiliation, deliberation, generation, presentation, classification, intimidation, vacation, calculation, qualification, formation, misinformation, infiltration, deforestation, sanctification, notation, indentation, orientation, magnification, elevation, annihilation, inhalation, exasperation, motivation, litigation, mutilation, invitation, regulations, revelation, sensation, ventilation, violation, abomination, acceleration, accommodation, approximation, cohabitation, contamination, cooperation, coordination, documentation, glorification.

Meditation

(Deep breath)
In this moment of relaxation
And contemplation
I experience a transformation
A fresh breeze of inspiration
Using my imagination
To transcend my situation
Filled with appreciation
And fascination for
Freedom's emancipation
This moment's exploration
Beyond limitations
Hatred's obliteration
No more irritation
Aggravation
Complications
Peace of mind is my journey's destination

Ation-Academic-Nation

School…
What an irritation!
It defies the imagination!
In math I mess up my multiplication equations.
English requires memorization.
And reading all sorts of publications
Writing about quotations
There's just too much information
If you ask your teacher
something for clarification,
they'll give you a long, drawn out explanation
Followed by an examination
Then pick on you for your Capitalization
Or wrong use of; punctuation…
And you don't dare lose your identification
Or forget to pay your library obligations,
They'll send you to the administration
Or they stick you in In-School-Suspension isolation

Flight School

You need to have full relaxation

To be in this situation

There are many manuals requiring memorization

You will be put through a simulation

You will feel frustration

Bombarded by lots of information

They will push you beyond your limitations

You will have to map out every destination

If you pull a high-g ejection
you may require hospitalization

But when you finish flight school,
you will have everyone's admiration

Surprise Ending Poems

Giving a poem a special twist with a surprise ending is not easy, but it can be fun. I recommend you beg them not to end with, "and then I woke up and found out it was just a dream." Silly or sensational, trying to come up with something that works makes one think and that's a vital part of learning: learning to think.

Example:

I kissed her lips, her cheek, her eyes

And told her my love for you never dies

I stroked her hair, I held her tight

And said, I'll sleep with you tonight

But not a word to me she said

Such a pity, she was dead

My First Time

The sky was dark, the moon still high

We were alone, her and I

Her eyes were brown as mine are too

There was only one thing left to do

I was new at this, but I tried my best

I put my hand upon her breast

Though I'm glad to say it's over now

My first time… milking a cow.

Holiday for One

We'd all like to have our fifteen minutes of fame; to be noticed, admired and appreciated. This poem is all about students celebrating themselves. In their poems, they are to describe a new holiday, named for them. They choose the date, and describe some of the rituals, customs or types of celebrations that are fitting for this marvelous occasion. This is a good time to explain and encourage hyperbole (extreme exaggeration) .

Aloha and welcome, students
    As most of you know
        this is teacher appreciation week

And today, mean old Monday is Mr. Martin's Day

You can all show your thanks
    by making this the best class ever

Creative minds
    and fun times

That's what I'd like to see
That's what I want this class to be

Deep thoughts, ideas shared

Work done well that shows you care
Respectful silences, gentle laughter
A sense of adventure: that's what I'm after

Friendships forged, good times had
A day when no one makes me mad

No one's cruel, no one's scheming
Someone wake me, I must be dreaming.

Another example:

My day

It's my day

High in the sky it is I day

Bow down in reverence

Compliment away

Treat me like royalty

This is my day

I get all the money

All the love is mine

Make me the center of attention

And the day will go just fine

You can have the other three-hundred sixty-four

Now give me all life's sweet things

I couldn't want for more

Alpha Poetry

For this format, students must stay with one topic and begin each line of their poem with a sequential letter of the alphabet. They don't have to start with "A" if they'd rather start in the middle somewhere and work their way around to it such as starting with "L" and ending twenty-six lines later with "K." For a variation on the format, they can use the letters in any order, but they must use them all. Give the kids a break when it comes to the letters X and Z such as being able to use words like eXactly or eXciting or falling asleep when they hit ZZZZZZZZZ. For an advanced challenge, there's Alphabet Soup: have the students pick ten letters (at random or from a hat) and create a poem of ten lines beginning with those letters. They have the option of using the letters in any order they choose, or staying with the order the letters are picked which is even harder. (I'd leave out the letters X and Z)

All my life, I've been writing poems
Beginning with high school days
Can't say it's hurt me none
Don't plan on stoppin' any time soon
Each poem is a memory, a part of me
Finding just the right phrase is my kind of fun
Gotta find the time to rhyme
Hard to believe it's been over forty years now
I enjoy free verse the best with internal rhyme
Just playing with sound and ideas
Kids like it because it's their thoughts and emotions
Love poems have helped me melt hearts
Memories return to me captured in the poetry
Now and then, I surprise myself
Originality means a lot to me
Poetry slams give me hope for our literary future
Quiet times are best for writing, to hear the sound inside
Reading poems we write is a form of publication
Spending time creating is time well spent
Teachers don't have to give poems grades, only applause
Use it or lose it: an imagination is a terrible thing to waste
Variety of poetry keeps things fresh and challenging
We be poets all, not know it alls
X-treme ideas at work
You never know what's coming next
Zip the lip, pick up the pen and let the poetry begin.

A is for Achieving
B is being the best
C is taking the challenge
D is for dreams and rest
E is for encouraging others
F for friends who understand
G is for good times together
H is for helping all you can
I is for intellect to guide you
J is for justice, that's fair
K is for kids, yes we're awesome
L is for leaders who care
M is for mothers who love us
N is no drugs and no smoking
O is this One Life we're given
P stands for peace, and I'm not joking
Q is the quiet inside us
R are relationships that heal
S is for summers and sailing
T is please teach us what's real
U is the University that accepts you
V are the values that guide us
W the water for our thirsting
X is the extreme love that's inside us
Y is You and I; Life is short, so:
Zoom. Zoom. Zoom!

Alphabet Soup example given the letters

HBTMSNALWTI

Humans think we're so great because we create

But wait…Humpback whales also create

They have songs

Most human kind songs are long gone,

Swallowed by history

No matter…the importance is song

And getting along

Like harmony

Would whales wage war under the sea?

That seems such a silly thing

Isn't it so much more fun to sing?

How Inviting

Write a poem inviting someone to join you for a special occasion.

All earth's children are invited

To a memorial service

This day of our good lord

For the burial of Mister War

May he rest in peace

A spaceship earth reception to follow

Please R.S.V.P.

        A.S.A.P.

The Society for the Preservation of Society

You are invited

To live with me always

Might as well make it official

You've been in my heart for some time now

I will marry you

Cherish you

Take care of you through thick and thin

Let's see how two become one

Let's go it together

And share all the fun

You are invited

Invited to stay

Because you are the best part

The best part of my day

"But" Changes Everything

Write a poem choosing several of the following starting suggestions. You may give more than one reason for each and you're always welcome to come up with your own ideas. These poems show the power of one simple word: "but". No one wants to hear "I love you, but…" (I like to call them "But Poems.")

I'd love to come to school but. . .

I love you but…

I would be rich and famous but. . .

I would've attended practice but. . .

I would have worked out but…

I would have gone to work but…

I would have gone to detention but…

I would have helped but…

I would have come to your party but…

I would have lost weight but…

I would have read a book but…

I would have done my chores but…

I would have gone to the mall but…

I would have given blood but…

I would have volunteered but…

I would have done my homework…

I would've seen a movie but…

I would have listened to my teacher but…

I would have been smarter but…

I would've got away with it but…

Our Buts

Hawaii's really nice but it's not going to stay like this forever

I'm starved but I can't eat 'cause I'm on a diet

I wish boys would like girls for who they are but some boys only go for good looks.

I'm in love, but not with you

I'm a good kid but not all the time

I may be dumb but I know a lot of stuff

Smoking isn't a sport, but if it was, would the first to die be the ones who win?

I want to stop the war but I don't know how

We could have peace on earth but people have to learn to get along

I could tell you more, but I don't have the time.

Buts About It

I would buy a Lamborghini
A Ferrari
And a Rolls Royce
But I have no money

I would date Jessica Alba,
Pamela Anderson, and J. Lo
But I'm a kid.

I would race in the Indy 500
But I don't know how to drive

I would go to the moon
But I have to go to sleep by ten

I would chase rhinos in Africa
But I have to feed my dog

I would be the president of the United States
But I've got 23 more years until I qualify

I've got a lot of ideas
But I guess they'll have to wait

Love You But

I love you but. . .
 I have no money
 I have someone else
 I'm not in love with you

I would have done my work but. . .
 I lost it
 My dog ate it
 My printer ran out of ink
 I left it at home
 It got wet
 My brother drew on it
 My mom spilt water over it

I want to be rich and famous but. . .
 I got fired
 I haven't got discovered yet
 I never got a diploma
 My parents wouldn't let me

I'm sorry I'm late but. . .

The traffic was backed up
I over slept
I had to drop off the kids
I was smoking crack

Thesaurus Poems

For these poems, students may take a poem they've already written then go to the thesaurus to look up synonyms to add to the poem.

I would be happy, no
     Cheerful, no
        Delighted to have you by my side
But you're not here
  You're missing,
    You're absent

I patiently await your arrival
  Your appearance,
    Your entrance
Still, I'm fearfully afraid that
  You may not show at all
    And then you'll never see
      My loving loyalty
        And dedicated devotion
And I would be lost, no
  Hurt, no
    Broken hearted

Because I'm Free

It's not easy to describe me

I'm not lazy, I'm kick back

I'm not egotistical, just totally cool

I'm not bad, I'm rad

I'm not short, just vertically challenged

I'm not dumb,
        just not the sharpest shovel in the shed

I'm not stressed, just high strung

    I'm no baby, just forever young

I'm not old fashioned, just proper

    Not overly handsome, I'm no show stopper

Not a player, just a ladies man

    Besides I'm still decidin' just who I'll be

        and who I am.

Work It

These poems are all about imagining careers. Students can write about their ideal job or different kinds of work they might experience as adulthood approaches. Doing a little in-depth thinking about what each sort of job entails can help them try it on for size, so to speak. Here's a listing of some occupations students can choose from (or pick their own favorites).

Teacher, Fireman, Police Officer, Mail Carrier, Computer Tech, Doctor, Lawyer, Judge, Model, Singer, Musician, Actor, Accountant, Marine Biologist, Scientist, Athlete, Television producer, Photographer, Lawn Maintenance, Auto Mechanic, Sales Person, Flight Attendant. Waiter, Pilot, Military, Electrician, Roadie, Journalist, Carpenter, Construction Worker, Truck Driver, Nurse, Chef, Rubbish Collector, Park Ranger, Architect, Engineer, Artist, Fashion Designer, Hair Stylist, Bus Driver, Race Car Driver, Farmer, Ranch Hand, Politician, Surfer, Lifeguard, Dishwasher, DJ, Fisherman, Business Owner, Masseuse, Preacher, Factory Worker, Merchant Mariner, Librarian, Painter, Logger, Reporter, Comedian.

Politician

My fellow Americans…

Whether you've declared yourself
    Democrat
    Republican
    Independent
    Uninspired or otherwise
Hold out
    Hoping for the day you'll vote through your TV
When the land of the free
    A government of the people and for the people
        Will ask the people to have a hand and a say
Hold out
    Hoping for the day
When we'll quit worrying why everything's a mess
    And start taking a guess at a better way

Hold on

        Hold out for the day

A Minister:

You can pray and preach
            Bow and chant
                Meditate and contemplate

You can climb mountains
        And sit surrounded by bird song breezes
                But please, don't walk away from love

You can talk to your friends
        e-mail everyone you know
        bounce ideas off satellites in space
        but don't forget to mention love wins

You can be rich and famous
            Envied and pampered
                Able to buy a slice of paradise
But my advice is to spend some time
                Looking for the loving thing

            Then sing, dance, sculpt, write
        and try to create more love
wherever you go
        however much you can
            no matter what you do
                    don't forget to love

Factory Worker:

Blue collar blues

    Ain't it sad news

So you curse the boredom

      The factory fatigue

        And wait for the weekend

          For a touch of intrigue

You drink oceans of coffee to keep sleep away

    And complain to the guys

          'bout how little you're paid

blue collar brown bagger

     and on my days off I stagger

     and try to forget that

         I'm nowhere

Letter Poems

Have the students write a poem that sounds like a letter to God, or a famous person, a family member, or a friend. They could pick out some person who has been inspirational in their life and write them a letter poem to show their gratitude, then actually mail it.

Dear Lord
Who art in heaven
Zip code cloud nine,

I just wanted to write
  To thank you for my life
    For all it has been and can be
      And I hope you're not mad at me

I know we haven't spoken in a while
  But lately, praying is not my style

Still, I honestly wish I knew you better
  And I would appreciate getting a letter from you
    Informing me exactly what you'd like me to do

But until I do, I guess I'll just continue…

    Faithfully yours,

<u>Dear Saint Pete, Pearly Gates,</u>

If death should arrive as a surprise
My life would become a list of should-have-dones…
                              Wish I saids…
                    Oh, God, no…not dead…not dead

I didn't hold my wife enough
        Didn't play in the rain enough
                Didn't travel far and wide
                        Didn't achieve peace inside

Didn't think enough
                Didn't care
Not death. Not now. It's not fair

I need to hike to the top of every mountain
        Float on my back in the salty sea
                Touch someone
                        Do something
                                Be free

No death…not me.

Please Saint Pete, take your time

Poetry Poem

Now that the students have learned some things about poetry, have them write a poem on the topic of poetry.

Why?

Why write?

Why bother to compose
the poetry and prose?

Hasn't somebody said it all before?

How can there be more to say?

And who would listen, anyway?

Might as well hang this poem up to dry

And never ask a poet, "Why?"

Whole Lotta Nothin'

If you write about nothin', nothin's what you get

'cuz nothin' comes from nothin'

at least it hasn't yet

You'll just be spinnin' your wheels

and you know how that feels

Too much head and not enough heart

Too soon it ends

it all depends

on what you say at the start

Nothin' ventured, nothin' gained

Nothin' left to do

Done startin'

I type my name: Rod Martin

<u>Understanding Poetry</u>

In relating to poetry,
whether you find it confusing…or not
You must see it and feel it, like a shivering hot
From the top of one's head, the words tumble down
Crumpled and broken and twisted around
Some slumping or soaring from tongue to mind's ear
A rhyme is developing, or so I do fear

Confined to a pattern? That's a waste of good time
Though darn it, the poem continues to rhyme
Now, let's have none of that. It's time to be free
And if you're following all this nonsense
you'll undoubtedly be
amused and confused, yes, it's all clear as mud
Like a curtained metaphor night that falls with a thud

So much for symbolism, but keep it in mind
It's not hard to write poems

if you don't try to rhyme.

What Poets Do

Oh, you know…
It may seem strange
The way I can rearrange words
To say something
Or nothing at all
Like scrawl on the wall if you will, and still,
The poet is free
No, I will not be confined by my commentary
Absolutely unrestrained
I'm a run-away train
Not a trained little dog in a circus
Not the least bit bound
I speak for the sake of sound
Bursting around your ear-bones
Like headphones filled with rock and roll
An imaginary stroll on a tightrope of time
And nonsense and rhyme
Just for you

Because that's what poets do.

The Poets Prayer

Now I sit me down to write

Before I go to sleep this night.

If I should die before I wake,

My penmanship's my least mistake.

Free Verse Abandon

Pencil Poem
       As in get the lead out
              And rhyme a few

 Now wouldn't you
       Like some sound
          Bouncing around your brain
Be it sweet refrain
       Or free verse abandon
          The random sound of rhyme
    Can Feel So
       Fine.

Why write?

Pressed to write
Stressed, uptight
Impressed? Alright

Who'd have guessed I might compose
                Words so free of prose?

Images that stand, though leaning
    In need of the support of meaning

Semantic flippery
    Catch my slippery drift?

                I am adrift in a sea of words

Gulping down mouthfuls of metaphor
    Washed up on the
    "someone's already done this" shore

Hang this poem
        Up to dry
            And remember
                Never ever
                    Ask a poet, "Why?"

<u>A poetry time</u>

Is playing with rhyme

Bouncing ideas off the mind

Like a juggling ball

That's all

It's a time to reflect and fly

To wonder "Why?"

And we thank you

For being a part

Bless your heart

Our art here performed for you

'cause that's what poets do

Now Just a Moment

Never a poem moment

At home moment in time

The rhyme is woven within

As I begin to play with sound

It's bound to confuse some

Ho hum for them

When words seem to fly

with a power of their own

and I am alone with my thoughts

this rhyme

A home poem moment in time.

Quiet, Please

I need quiet to write
    Early morning or late at night
A time with no one else around
    To hear the sound in my head
                    instead
              of the clatter chatter
        that is my life

No kids
No friend
No wife
Just my thoughts
     this poem
       and me

I want words to stumble
    Tripping off the tongue, alright?
         Any quiet time of night or day
             Just let me play
          With the sound
        Of words
      Their rhythm
    Their rhyme
Oh, give me quiet time

And though inspiration would be nice

    Sometimes
    Silence
    Will suffice

Words

There are plenty of words
In poems
In books
Famous and infamous
And not the least famous
    Not printed,
        Published
        Perused
Words
Poems
Poets able to overflow fountains of feelings
        Mountains of memories and metaphor
           Acres of images and imaginings
Yes, imagine
        The wonder of words
           Like particles of light
That illuminate the mind
           The page

This is good stuff
You have my word

New News

Have the students look for an unusual/interesting news story from the newspaper or a news magazine and use that as inspiration for a poem. The students may want to write from the point of view of someone involved in that news event.

The Pres Says

The time has come
(what took us so long?)
To reaffirm our enduring spirit;
(enduring's easy, living's tougher)
To choose our better history;
(Don't historians always choose?)
To carry forward that precious gift
(Forward is as good a direction as any)
That noble idea:
(And it's a good idea)

That all are equal
(I know I am)

All are free
(Workin' on it)

And all deserve a chance to pursue
their full measure of happiness
(Happy to hear it)

(The following is also an example of "Ation" poetry)

<u>Ode to Paris</u>

Paris Hilton's sophistication
Is just so much constipation

Likes to see her name in all those publications
Queen of the quotation confirmation

Super socialite of every situation
Skinny ninny navel inny kind of starvation

You go girl with your sexy sensual sensations
Who cares if you can carry on a conversation

Spokes-girl from the wannabe generation
Tabloid trailer trash or rich kid creation

A mortification of media saturation
Been to jail, found God, sort of transformation
It's all about your fan's fanatical fascination

Famous for being famous doesn't earn my admiration

Get a life, little girl
That's my recommendation.

The students can also just make up poems that sound like they're from a newspaper article:

Obituary

George Hawkins

> Three small kids

> One good wife

April sixteenth, took his life

> Tears were shed

> Some sent regrets

Yet, given time, everyone forgets

> Love me, if you will

> Hate me, if you must

> Ashes to ashes

> Dust to dust

Time Travel

Time travel poems are concerned with the past, present and future of our world. The students have their choice of which time frame to write about. If they choose to deal with the past, they can do so in two different ways: they can write as if they were born in some era of the past, from the point of view of people in that time or they can compose their poem as if they are a time traveler visiting the past but retaining their knowledge of our modern day world. The same twist can be used for the future: they write as if that's just the world they know, or they are visitors from our present time or even the past. In dealing with the present, perhaps they could be a "time transporter" who has brought some famous person from the past to our modern day world with the help of their trusty time machine. Would Galileo be honored to have space probes named after him? Would Abraham Lincoln enjoy talking politics with Barack Obama? This assignment could first be written in prose form and then edited to become poetry. It lends itself to imaginative thinking and the imagination is where new ideas and dreams come from.

Time Traveler me

I can't wait to see?

Is Armageddon gonna get us?

Or is it our fate
    to wither away
        under clouds of loose atoms of a nuclear nature
The Earth could lose the gravitational tug of war
    with her celestial sisters and go spinning off into space

Pollution will most likely be the ultimate solution to
overpopulation: that stuff can kill you

Wouldn't it be wild if the human race
had to battle scientifically controlled and created
nifty new diseases?
Global warming or ice age chill

It's gotta end, I'm sure it will

The sun could grow too big or love too small

It could end in a bang or a whimper
       or it might not end at all
I'll let you know when I return in the Fall.

NYC

If the prophets had seen New York
Their weeping would not have been for Jerusalem
To see our world as it is today
Might hurt their hearts
Take their breath away
Manhattan's millions
Multitudes to meet but never know
    Ladies of the street
        Selling themselves like so much meat
            Same as in the days of old
    But with so much more skin to show
And of course, there will still be drunks
Villains of the vine
    Who start something hurting inside me
Jesus said, "I was a drunk in a doorway
    And you shook your head
        And never asked
Why must the world be this way?"
Could the prophets truly predict this day
Or do things never change
    Just a bit more strange
Then I saw your picture, J.C.
    In glorious three-D
Selling beside a sex toy in some store window
Wicked city
    With no prophets left to stone
Why should God destroy you, Big Apple of knowledge
    When you seem to be doing that on your own.

Dying Keeps It Real

Most people will admit that dying is just a part of life. Consider also, that if we didn't die, life as we know it would be so different. Life would lose some of its excitement, its urgency. Knowing our breaths are limited makes breathing beautiful. Thinking or writing about death doesn't mean one is suicidal. Perhaps we are just curious, since death is a great unknown. I wouldn't force this topic on the kids, but if they're up for the challenge, give them the chance. They can contemplate their own mortality or write about the loss of a loved one or pet. They can imagine how it feels to die in battle, or from an illness. This can help promote empathy for the suffering of others.

Gonna die someday

Might die soon

　　Who can say

　　　　And should I live for years

　　　　　　Full years

　　If nothing should go wrong

　　　　And I live long

And don't worry

And don't hurry death

With my last breath

I might reincarnate

Or Pearly Gate

But I can't wait to see

If death will wait for me

WHY WAR?

Why war?
Is that really what we're here for?
In this age of complexity,
why maintain such misery?
Aren't we long past the day?
Boys, put your war toys away. And learn to play.

I didn't volunteer to fight and die
    because I stopped to question, "why?"

What can we say to the honored dead?
  Those who fought and bled.
    What pardon is left unsaid?

When the battles on and the bullets fly,
the boys on both sides pray, "Don't let me die."

Somewhere a mother cries for a lost son.

War isn't worth it.

War isn't fun.

They Asked Me

They asked me to go to war

I feel I have to go

and if I die

all of my family will cry

But I wonder who will wonder, "why?"

Was it worth the sacrifice?

Fighting for freedom in this foreign land

Where I left my legs behind

And I still don't understand

Hunting

If I was a deer, fleeting away at a run

Would you be a hunter, behind a hunter's gun?

If I was a heart beating in fright

Would you be a bullet burning in flight?

If death found its mark and decided to stay

Would you pick up your gun and be off on your way?

Surprise

If death should arrive

     As a surprise
Life becomes a list of should-have-dones…
          Wish I saids…

Oh, God, no…not dead…not dead

I didn't hold my wife enough
Didn't play in the rain enough
Didn't travel far and wide
Didn't achieve peace inside

Didn't think enough
     Didn't care

Not death. Not now. It's not fair

I need to hike to the top of every mountain
Float on my back in the salty sea
Touch someone
Do something
Be free

No death…not me.

The Beauty That is Being

Perhaps I might

    Pass death by

And forsaking heavenly custom,

    Melt into cool laser light

Flowing into patterned colors

    Black space

      And shining stars

        The beauty that is being

    A child playing with light

    At night

Figuratively Speaking

Give the students a listing of several phrases that qualify as figurative language and ask them to create a poem using at least three (with the correct meaning or context).

Figurative Language examples to choose from:

Wet behind the ears: and inexperience person

You don't know beans: to know nothing about a topic.

You're putting the cart before the horse: you have the order of things reversed.

One horse town: a small, quiet town.

Raining cats and dogs: hard, pouring rain.

That don't hold water: something that is not true.

Your Achilles heel: your area of weakness.

By hook or crook: by one means or another, fair of fowl.

Carrying coals to Newcastle: like selling refrigerators to Eskimos.

In hot water: in trouble.

I got hauled over the coals: reprimanded severely (yelled at).

Big shot: a person of importance.

The lions share: the biggest amount of some prize or reward.

To learn the ropes: to become familiar with the details of how to do something.

To split hairs: to argue of small points.

To spill the beans: to tell a secret too soon.

You're barking up the wrong tree: You're on the wrong course of action.

Left holding the bag: Got stuck with some unwanted task or blamed for some wrong-doing.

Out of the frying pan and into the fire: to go from one problem to a worse one.

The apple of my eye: the one I hold dearest.

To get caught flat footed: caught unprepared.

To fly the coop: to escape or play hooky.

Through thick and thin: through good times and bad.

Playing second fiddle: not having the lead position.

Keep the ball rolling: keep the interest for something going.

A wild goose chase: a goal or pursuit that is worthless, wasting your time.

Greasing someone's palm: giving them money in exchange for favors.

Bring down the house: to have a hit show the audience loves.

Hold your horses: keep cool and be patient.

To run something into the ground: Carry something to extremes.

A month of Sundays: a long time.

To pull the wool over someone's eyes: to fool them.

I'll keep my fingers crossed: wishing you good luck.

Keep it under your hat: keep it a secret.

I got it straight from the horses mouth: I got the information from the highest source.

Faster than greased lightning: very fast.

Chip off the old block: a kid who is like his or her parent.

By the skin of my teeth: just barely, by a narrow margin.

Behind the eight ball: to be in trouble.

Wolf in sheep's clothing: a bad guy who appears to be good, but isn't.

Don't let the cat out of the bag: don't tell the secret.

In the nick of time: at the critical or precise moment.

He's got a chip on his shoulder: he wants to fight about something.

Don't burn the candle at both ends: don't try to do too much in one day and wear yourself out.

Take it with a grain of salt: to remain doubtful or skeptical.

To get someone's goat: to annoy or tease them, get them upset.

So Much To Do

Burning the candle at both ends
Dividing myself between family and friends
So much to do and so little time
Got to get things done while I'm in my prime
From early morning until late at night
Taking what's left and making it right
Planning the future, making up for the past
I hope I can make it, I hope I can last

Figuratively Full

Honey, I ain't seen you in a month a Sundays

Since you run off to that big city

Sayin' you gotta paddle your own canoe

Your Aunty Bessy done spilled the beans

about you getting in some hot water

      with some big shot up North
Honey you was barkin' up the wrong tree with that one

He was a wolf in sheep's clothing

Them kind of men like burnin' the candle at both ends

Hear tell he had you playing second fiddle

Then he flew the coop and left you holdin' the bag

      But that is a mighty cute baby.

PSA Poetry

Encourage your students to pick an issue of importance to them a then create a brief poem that could become a video public service announcement.

Example:

Crystal Meth/Ice

Ice princess
Dressed to kill
Chills your heart
And holds you still
Frozen hopes attack your will
You're addicted to the thrill
Until all the world's a muffled hush
Living for that sudden rush
Your mind a tattered tapestry
icy eyes that never see
Unraveling paranoia
Then finally
You grow cold
Before you grow old

<u>Another example:</u>

<u>Don't Do Drugs</u>

Don't do drugs
You nic-fit nitwit you're gonna burn your bed

It's not worth the high
Find better things to do with your head

Crack and cocaine
Why you tryin' to fry your brain?

You monkey 'round with smack
And that monkey's gonna ride your back

Shootin' up speed, you might catch somethin'
That you don't need

You got your ups, your downs, your PCP:
Why not just pass 'em by

If you're a slave to a habit
then you're not free.

Vantage Point Poems

Have the students choose a specific location in the classroom or around the school and write a poem describing things they see from that particular vantage point. Then have them give their poem to one of their classmates and see if he or she can find that exact spot. It's all in the details. The more specific details the poet gives, the easier it will be to find that spot.

A view from the international space station

I live in a nation of light

    Seen from space, it shines at night

From the aura of brave souls lost in freedom's fight

    To the spark of first love, youth's delight

We've shown the world

    there's more to power than might

        our lives shape the planet

           let's hope we do it right

(The Beach)

I love going surfing

And swimming in the water

Feeling of sand between my toes

Snorkeling

Boogey boarding

Spear fishing

Building sand castles

And lying in the water playing dead

Some folks stayed glued to their video screens

Give me this place instead

From My Car

When driving behind a slow-go Honda

Shiny black

Something caught my eye

Right there on the back

A serenade of trees and sky

In this moving mirror, whizzing by

Again, amazed by what I did spy

Look and See

For this assignment, students are challenged to see things with the eyes of a poet. They must be consciously aware that they are looking for something special to write about. Seek and you will find.

Example:

Just A Stream

As I was heading for school, girls and boys

I rode across a ribbon of white noise

And though you might say it's just a stream

Please allow me this poet's dream

My goal is simply to make you think

And that's some of the finest water you'll ever drink

A Blessed Mist

I am lucky to see
    I must remember this

Today I found myself
    Surrounded by a blessed mist
A blessing rain that falls
    With such grace and ease

Gently revealing the morning breeze
Accentuated by sunlight as the new day starts
With a message of peace for our human hearts

Another example:

My Mountain Cove

Beauty? I can have my fill
Just by walking up my hill
Surrounded by my mountain cove
In this place I've come to love
So search for me up in the hills
I tell you, it still gives me chills
And I'd love to show this sight to you
"Cause there's nothing like a mountain view

Movement Poem

Have the students, walk, drive, swim, skateboard, jog, hike, or bike, recording their experiences and feelings in poetic form while doing the activity or immediately afterwards.

Driving behind a slow-go Honda
Shiny black
Something caught my eye
Right there on the back
A serenade of trees and sky
In this moving mirror, whizzing by
Again, amazed by what I did spy

Mr. Martin, where you been?
He said the answer is blowing in the wind
And today I saw things I never saw before
I watched a wild chicken soar
I saw the sun come over the hill
To ride along is such a thrill
To accelerate into the sun
I love my bike, it's so much fun
And so I'll tell you once again
The answer is blowin' in the wind.

Poem From A Hat

" Words, words, words"

Students are given 8-10 small pieces of paper and asked to write two nouns, two adjectives, two verbs, and two words from the dictionary: one per piece of paper. This is a good time to review those parts of speech.

Collect them and place in a box, or hat. (You may combine the student suggestions from other classes as well for a larger selection.)

Instructions to students: 1. Take out a piece of paper and label it "Words, words, words." include your name date and period. 2. Pick fifteen words from the hat. 3. Use ten of those words to create a poem and be sure to underline the words that came from the hat. 4. Include a simile or metaphor in the poem and underline it as well. 5. Use no more than two of the "hat words" per sentence or line. 6. You may use a form of the word. (for example, if the word is happy, you may use happiness). 7. Return the words to the hat when you're finished, check your writing, then turn it in.

Example: Use the following words in a poem: Freedom, work, fire, memories, cautious, inspiration, slow, and create.

Caution

Caution

Words at <u>work</u>

<u>Creating</u> connections

Carved in conscious momentary <u>memory</u>

Words like: <u>Freedom</u>

That can valiantly <u>inspire</u>

Start a fire

Or <u>slowly</u> expire

If

Left

Unsaid

Poems for your pets

Ask the students to write a poem about one or more of their pets. If they have none, they should imagine what it might be like to have a pet.

Puppy Poem

So many shoes, So little time
How I love this dog of mine

Though she will chew me out of house and home
At least I'll never be alone

We will have years to play
Boyish fun and doggy days

I'll walk her and she'll walk me
An exercise plan that's fun and free

For now, it's puppy love 'cause she's so cute
"Hey, has anyone seen my left boot?"

For Beauregard Bowser D. Dog

Doggone
My dog
You better not die
And I'll tell you why

I have invested big bucks
It operations and medications to improve your situation

So don't you tell me
That for my every year, you live three or four or more

I've heard it all before
But refuse to believe in a life without your company

Darn dog

You mean a lot to me

In Parting or Passing

You may have heard the phrase, "famous last words." Well, this is your students' opportunity to say goodbye to life as they know it. They may be moving half way around the globe, or traveling to another planet, or about to succumb to a deadly, incurable virus that attacks teenagers. In any case, they're going and it's time to say their good byes, to offer thanks, to beg forgiveness, to clear the slate, and to hope for better things ahead.

Example:

Wish I Had

If death should arrive
       As a surprise
Life becomes a list of should-have-dones…
              Wish-I- saids…

Oh, God, no…not dead…not dead

I didn't hold my wife enough
Didn't play in the rain enough
Didn't travel far and wide
Didn't achieve peace inside

Didn't think enough
          Didn't care

Not death. Not now. It's not fair

I need to hike to the top of every mountain
Float on my back in the salty sea
Touch someone
Do something
Be free

No death…not me.

Another example:

    <u>The Great Out There</u>

As I prepare

    To leave this earth

For the great out there

To explore

To know more

Should I not return

Don't pity me

For I will have learned

If man is suited for space

Or should we remain in our place?

We shall see.

I'm off.

Lucky me.

On Moving to Alaska

Sorry friends

I must me going

To the land where I hear it's always snowing

And blowing and cold

Or so I am told

But if you will just write

I can make it through the endless night

Poetic Dialogues:

Ask your students to write poems that are made up of two voices talking together, with no descriptive lines.

Dad: You kids don't know how lucky you are these days.
Kid: Whatever you say, Dad.

Dad: And you should stay home more instead of always out running around.
Kid: Don't you want me to have friends?

Dad: You could get a job, you know.
Kid: I thought you wanted me home?

Dad: If you don't like the rules in this house, you can get out.
Kid: It won't be long. I got accepted to that college I wanted.

Dad: And what did you make for dinner?
Kid: I love you too, Dad.

Up To You

Me: Alright, students, I've got a question for you: what's up? I'm not asking how you're doing? I'm asking what do you know about the word, "Up?" It's got a lot of meanings.

Them: Leave it to the creators of the English language to take a two letter word and give it multiple meanings.

Me: Don't blame us English teachers. We just try to make sense of this crazy stuff.

Them: What does a person want you to do when they say, "Speak up?" Talk to the clouds?

Me: And what about food? First you work up an appetite, then you warm up some left-overs, then you have to eat them all up, and then you have to clean up after yourself.

Them: That's a lot of "up" going down there.

Me: Here's two things you kids are good at: stirring up trouble…and thinking up excuses.

Them: Why do you lock up a house and lock down a prison?

Me: Are there any athletes in the house? Can you explain something to me? What do you do when you "Get up for the game"? What does that mean?

Them: There's ups all over.

Me: Well, our time is up so we're gonna wrap this up and if you didn't take notes for the up-coming test on this lecture: make something…up.

<u>It's About Time</u>

Have the students write about a specific time of day: dawn, the golden light of early morning, high noon, the afternoon, sunset, dusk, moonrise, midnight, or the wee hours of the morning. If possible, suggest they do that writing at that particular time. They might also enjoy just writing about the concept of time altogether. They might want to explore the meaning of some of the following phrases about time: Time will tell, Time has passed him/her by, Time flies when you're having fun, Take a time out, When your time is up, All the time in the world, Bide your time, In the nick of time, Time on my hands, Time heals all wounds, Time is money, Time and tide waits for no man, and Time stood still.

Off At a Run

Seconds race by

Human race by the time our day is done

we fall at the feet of forever

begging for but a few moments more

'til…

BANG goes the gun

Off at a run
Chasing each moment by racing each moment

And it's gone

No time to mourn it

From the day you're born it's a contest with time

Find the reason, the rhyme

Though you run 'til you ache with each step you take

Desiring it

Expiring it

Each second you take up

Can never be made up

So cherish your space in the race, human

Captured

The greatest thought
    I'll ever write
Could be these words
    This night
Not tomorrow's thought
    Or memories past
Just this moment
    Made to last

Your soft touch
    This tender kiss
      Just this

This poem
This rhyme
This moment in time
Captured

Mine.

<u>There's something 'bout the morning sun</u>
The golden blaze of rays
that come splashing up across the green
To brighten up the nature seen

Birds that fly through a gilded sky
Each etched-out ridge of the mountain side

As life wakes up to greet the day
With unuttered prayers for peace on earth

That glorious day
When the morning sun
paints the world with gold

breathing life into every hope we hold

someday we'll all shine like the morning sun

and live in peace

and love as one.

About Time

It's about time
There when I arrived
There when I leave
It exists as do I
As long
And longer
Than I
Motion follows upon motion
Flowing
Even flying
Past
Fast
Rarely slow
And I know
There is something I still must do
Will there be time
Time will be there
I hope
Or why waste the time
To live
To grow old
And grow wise
And grow young

Party Poem

Ask your students to describe a party with a special guest of honor. That special guest can be any famous person they'd like to meet, even a person from history such as Lincoln, Cleopatra, or Jesus.

Lincoln in the Land of Aloha

Honest Abe came to my party
A mixed race affair
I tell you the place was hoppin'
Seemed like everybody was there

There we Blacks and Whites, Indians, Hispanics
Even some French folk from across the Atlantic

Hawaiians, Filipinos, Puerto Ricans and Chinese
Russians, the Dutch, Swiss and Japanese

Abe was really impressed by such a diverse crowd
with enough racial harmony to make a President proud

So tell all your friends, your cousins, your momma
They should have seen Honest Abe's face,
when we all told him about Obama.

Christ Came Down

Christ came down this Christmas

    And saw us singing

        About someone called Santa

Buying booze and

Chasing chicks

Decorating trees

And letting the world go hungry

A tear came to his eye

And he wondered was it worth being born

        to die?

Spoonerisms

Legend has it that Professor Spooner started mixing up the words in his lectures to keep his student's attention. Your students may have fun with it as well. The trick to it is to switch the beginning sounds of two words in a phrase. The poems don't have to be long, and don't have to rhyme and it takes some experimentation to find the words that sound the best with their beginnings switched. Enjoy.

In the story "Goldilocks and the Three Bears"
It seems the <u>Boor Pears</u> were caught unawares
By a <u>Gittle Lirl</u> to decided to <u>Pesstrass</u>
She really was a naughty lass
But it sure was funny when Baby Bear said,
"Someone's been <u>Beeping</u> in my <u>Sled</u>."

Rindercella

Once aton a pime, there lived a young lady named Rindercella
She lived with her mean old mep stother
And her two sisty uglers
They made Rindercella do all the wordy dirk
While they just sat around chocking eatlets
And magging readazines
One day, while Rindercella was flopping the moor
The two sisty unglers came in and said

The pransome hintz is giving a bancy fall
And we're invited!
But you can't go (ah)
So Rindercella went into the kitchen
With ties in her ears
When suddenly, there was a blinding lash of flight
And who should appear but a fuitable berry
Who are you,
And what do you want?, asked Rindercela
And the fuitable berry said,
I'm your Merry Fod Gother
And I've come to want you a grish
Well, gee, all I want to do is bo to the gall
And meet the Pransome Hintz
That's a pretty wough tish but K-O
And FOOP!
That's poof backwards…
Rindercella was transformed into a bavishing rooty
She had on a long gatin sown
A necklace of poobies and rearls
And on her feet, two tiny sas glippers
Now you may go to the ball, Rindercella
But you must be clock by twelve O home
Soon she cast to the camel
But who were the first two people she met?
The two sisty uglers!
But Rindercella was so good looking
They didn't even cinderize Reckignella
Then she met the Pransome Hintz
He said, may I dave this hance?
Why you, you're boopsalootly aptiful

More beautiful than Beeping Slooty
But just as he was about to ask
For her mare in handage
Rindercella looked up at the clock and said,
It's the moke of stridnight!
And she ban from the rall.
But when she did, she slopped her dripper
I mean, dripped her slopper
Dropped her slipper

The Pransome Hintz picked it up and said
If I can just find the woman
whose soot this flipper flits
I'll know with whom I've lallen in fove

So, the next house he went from day to day
Until he came to the sin where Housedarella lived
He docked on the knor
But who should open the door
but the two sisty uglers!

He tried the slipper on them
But of course, their beet were too fig

But when Rindercella tried it
The flipper pitted serfectly

They were married
And hap lividly ever after.

Little Head Lightning Rod

Little Rat Rotten Hut
Lived with her mother
At the fedge of a deep dark orest
Morn one-ing, mer hother said.
"Little Hood Letting Ride,
Cook these takies
And go grand your visit-mother
but don't stalk to trangers."
"Ok, dother mear"...and off she was

As little Head Lightning Rod was falking in the worest
Come should who along but a wolfed wick.
"Go are you where-ing Little Hood Riding Red?"
"I'm going to grand my visit mother and cook her these
bring-ies"
"And are you going to stop and flower her some picks?" asked
the wolf.
"Good idea!"
So while Little Rat Rotten Hut was flicking powers, the neaky
swolf grand ahead to ran-mother's house and was just about to
up her gobble, but clocked her in the losette instead when he
heard Riddle Led approaching.
The wolf grabbed one of grandmother's bonnets and tied one on.
When Rittle Led wolfed the saw, she said,
"Grandmother, what big eyes you have!"

"The better to dear you with, my see," said the wolf.
"But grandmother, what big ears you have!"
The better to dear you with, my hear.
"Grand but-mother, what big teeth you have!"
"Eat with you the better to!" cried the wolf
beaping from the led.
And Little Head Lightning Rod screamed so loud that a hassling punter, or was it a passing hunter, screamed her heards and cost into the burst-age. The neaky swolf backed out the leap door and Little Rat Rotten Hut was saved! Why? Because she had a big mouth, and she wasn't afraid to use it. And the storal of the mory is Don't stalk to trangers 'cause seems aren't always what they thing.

Poetry of Negativity

The main focus of this style of poem is not to describe a situation, but to tell what it's not like. Another approach would be to look for the negative, what's wrong with things in your life or the world, though the teacher can request it end with some positive twist.

No she's not...

No she's not,
Nice like you say,

No she's not,
Fun in that way,

No she's not,
Sharp as a knife,
No she's not,
Larger than life,

No she's not,
Cute as can be,

No she's not,
What you all see,

No she's not,
She's so much more,

But now she's not mine
Like she was before

Negativity Gone Glad

I'm surrounded by chaos
A world where there's never enough
                        Never enough time
                    Never enough money
                Not nearly enough love
A world with mounting problems
                    Millions of people
            Multiple warheads
Raunchy politicians
        Rampant pollution
                Runaway inflation
                        Infatuation with fortune and fame
Fortunately for me,
                I can find a calm center
            in this turbulent sea of humanity
The center of me
        just a breath away
                and I am set free
                        to consider not just what is
                                but what can be

There's children's laughter even in Ghettos
and flowers have been known
        to push their way through pavement to bloom

Within this silence,
    whispers of worship can be heard
It is safe here for the Creator and creation to commune
        To come together as one
                    One heart

            And that's where the fun starts

Bang or a Whimper (Negative with a twist)

Some say
        The world will end

    In an atomic recreation of the original big bang

A global death wish come radioactive reality

        Compliments of a money hungry

                military industrial complex

The world could choke on smog or vog

            Or perish under an age of ice

Fire would suffice

        But take my advice

It may not end at all,

So we might as well live
        with our children's children in mind.

What's This County Coming To?

Politicians lying.

Babies dying.

Poverty wherever you go.

What's this country coming to?

I just don't know.

Crack, Abuse, AIDS.

Kids cutting themselves with razor blades!

You can't drink the water
Don't dare breathe the air

Land of the free and equality
Does anyone care?

No peace overseas.
No peace at home.

Maybe, kids, it's safer
Not even being born.

Nature's Poetry

Nature's beauty has been a major topic of poems since the genre began. Have students pick from the following list or come up with their own topic relating to something in nature, from a mountain range to bit of moss; something that sparks their interest or a hidden memory.

<u>Some topics to choose from:</u>

The Ocean, Waves, Swimming, Mountains, Hiking, Trees, Flowers, Animals, Insects, Birds, Reptiles, Sunshine, Clouds, Wind, Rain, Sand.

Earth, Rivers, Waterfalls, Sunsets, Sun, Sun-showers, Shadows, Streams, Space, Beaches, Hurricanes, The Seasons, Sailing, Diving, Snow, Lightning, Stars, Kayaking, Fishing, Camping, Fire.

The scent of flowers on the breeze. The sound of a brook. The taste of honey or fresh fruit. The touch of a misty rain on your eyelashes. Fish lazing along a shoreline. The view from a mountain top. Skating on thin ice. Trees bent low by crystal covering of icy rain. Sinking into snow-banks. Catching snowflakes on your tongue. The many uses for wood. Bamboo rattling in a strong wind.

Desert

Desert, I don't know you
Like you know dust storms and gullies
Dry river beds and rice grass
Geologically-fixed rainbows
And rainstorms that never reach the ground
Yes, and the sound <u>no</u> water makes
When it isn't helping things live

Brave, thirsty souls have labored on your stage/plateau
Where did they go?
What have you done with them, desert?
Did vultures see and partake?
Is it a mistake to rent from a sandstone tenement?

Coyotes and owls
Star-filled nights when the moon allows
Creatures that can scurry and leap without sound
Hungry eyes are watching

Thirsty days are coming
Think thin and dig in
Into the desert
And sleep with one ear awake
To rain

Sand

Sand is more
       Than something that sneaks
               Into sneakers
      Is sifted through fingers
     Plastered in castles
It is a massive amount of water
          Showing boulders who's boss
    The futile battle of stone to remain together
It's a highway at low tide
    A moving hill
        Jogging path and moldable bed
      Young minds museum playground
It's little chunks of rock, coral and shells
      And other erosion resistant minerals
It's crunchy in oatmeal
      Palatable on peanut butter and jelly
        Not so spicy in soup
But basically, it's all over everything
               at the beach
it's amazing
it's where sea kisses earth
union
shifting alliances and illusions

the softest of stone

The Right Kind of Noise

The first time ever I heard silence
    Not that the world stood still
        But it was the right kind of noise

Early morning river rapids
    And the sound of sunshine through branches

I stretch in my homemade hammock
        A drowsy rebirth

Oh yes, I've tasted freedom
And heard the way the world wakes in the morning

I've lived close to the earth
        Like a river
    With a feeling of flowing

            Knowing why I'm here

And the silence
      For once
          Was inside me

My Friend's Back Yard

A flutter by

In frolic flight

If wish you may

Then wish you might

Wish for peace on earth

A peace so dear

Now, look around

It's here.

It's here!

Lava Flow

Lava
Flowing down the volcano
Liquid land seeking out the sea
To sizzle
To harden
Or explode into razor sharp sand
New land
Barren and black
Wrinkled
Frozen puddles of pitch black brittle stone
And then
The first ferns take hold
And Ohia trees begin to grow
Grasses seed in the sandy cracks and crevices
eventually
through rain and wind
shadow and shade
death and decay
moss and mold
the forest unfolds its layer of life
its blanket of green comfort
for Nature's peaceful sleep
forest deep
forged in fire of lava love.

For A New You

This poem is all about making resolutions; whether it's a new year or new you. For this poem, the students make three resolutions starting out small and getting more serious, adventurous, or tackling something of great importance. After each of the three resolutions, they should make some comments about how they might go about making that resolution happen.

I'm Gonna Do It

I'm going to floss more

Even though the dentist cleans my teeth twice a year
it's still a pain
when salty beef jerky
gets stuck between my teeth
and it's embarrassing
     when you eat corn on the cob
and find out later when you smile you look silly

I'm going to love more

Because I think I'm too selfish sometimes
     And it might help me be more popular at school
And besides, it's in the Bible
and if I call myself a Christian,
     I better try and do what Jesus said.

I'm going to try to do something for others

Like serve meals at the homeless shelter
Or collect money for a charity
Or clean up litter at a park or playground
Or help old ladies across the street
I'd like to do something,
Even if it's only doing the dishes
Mom would like that

Not Out Of My Way

My resolution
          Is to make restitution
To every person, place and institution
          I may have wronged
                    In any way
When I can find a free day
     And it's not out of my way
          Not too high a price to pay for livin'
Given I've been given so much

Guess countin' my blessin's
          a life-long lesson

Story Poems

Read The Highwayman by Alfred Noyes for the students to show them how a poem can tell a story and challenge them to write their own story poems, (they don't have to be pages long).

Alfred Noyes (1880-1958)

The Highwayman

PART ONE

I

The wind was a torrent of darkness among the gusty trees,
The moon was a ghostly galleon tossed upon cloudy seas,
The road was a ribbon of moonlight over the purple moor,
And the highwayman came riding—
      Riding—riding—
The highwayman came riding, up to the old inn-door.

II

He'd a French cocked-hat on his forehead, a bunch of lace at his chin,
A coat of the claret velvet, and breeches of brown doe-skin;
They fitted with never a wrinkle: his boots were up to the thigh!
And he rode with a jewelled twinkle,

His pistol butts a-twinkle,
His rapier hilt a-twinkle, under the jewelled sky.

III

Over the cobbles he clattered and clashed in the dark inn-yard,
And he tapped with his whip on the shutters,
but all was locked and bared,
He whistled a tune to the window, and who should be waiting there
But the landlord's black-eyed daughter,
Bess, the landlord's daughter,
Plaiting a dark red love-knot into her long black hair.

IV

And dark in the dark old inn-yard a stable-wicket creaked
Where Tim the ostler listened; his face was white and peaked;
His eyes were hollows of madness, his hair like mouldy hay,
But he loved the landlord's daughter,
The landlord's red-lipped daughter,
Dumb as a dog he listened, and he heard the robber say—

V

"One kiss, my bonny sweetheart, I'm after a prize to-night,
But I shall be back with the yellow gold before the morning
light;
Yet, if they press me sharply, and harry me through the day,
Then look for me by moonlight,
Watch for me by moonlight,

I'll come to thee by moonlight, though hell should bar the
way."

VI

He rose upright in the stirrups; he scarce could reach her hand,
But she loosened her hair i' the casement! His face burnt like
a   brand
As the black cascade of perfume came tumbling over his
breast;
And he kissed its waves in the moonlight,
          (Oh, sweet, black waves in the moonlight!)
Then he tugged at his rein in the moonliglt, and galloped
away to the West.

PART TWO

I

He did not come in the dawning; he did not come at noon;
And out o' the tawny sunset, before the rise o' the moon,
When the road was a gypsy's ribbon, looping the purple moor,
A red-coat troop came marching—
          Marching—marching—
King George's men came matching, up to the old inn-door.

II

They said no word to the landlord, they drank his ale instead,
But they gagged his daughter and bound her to the foot of her

narrow bed;
   Two of them knelt at her casement, with muskets at their side!
   There was death at every window;
          And hell at one dark window;
For Bess could see, through her casement, the road that *he* would
ride.

III

   They had tied her up to attention, with many a sniggering
jest;
   They had bound a musket beside her, with the barrel
beneath her breast!
   "Now, keep good watch!" and they kissed her.
        She heard the dead man say—
Look for me by moonlight;
       Watch for me by moonlight;
I'll come to thee by moonlight, though hell should bar the way!

IV

She twisted her hands behind her; but all the knots held
 good!
   She writhed her hands till her fingers were wet with sweat or blood!
   They stretched and strained in the darkness, and the hours crawled
by like years,
   Till, now, on the stroke of midnight,
        Cold, on the stroke of midnight,
The tip of one finger touched it! The trigger at least was hers!

V

The tip of one finger touched it; she strove no more for the
rest!

Up, she stood up to attention, with the barrel beneath her
breast,

She would not risk their hearing; she would not strive again;

For the road lay bare in the moonlight;

  Blank and bare in the moonlight;

And the blood of her veins in the moonlight throbbed to her
love's refrain.

VI

Tlot-tlot; tlot-tlot! Had they heard it? The horse-hoofs ringing
clear;

Tlot-tlot, tlot-tlot, in the distance? Were they deaf that they did not
hear?

Down the ribbon of moonlight, over the brow of the hill,

The highwayman came riding,

  Riding, riding!

The red-coats looked to their priming! She stood up, straight
and still!

VII

Tlot-tlot, in the frosty silence! *Tlot-tlot,* in the echoing night!

Nearer he came and nearer! Her face was like a light!

Her eyes grew wide for a moment; she drew one last deep
breath,

Then her finger moved in the moonlight,

  Her musket shattered the moonlight,

Shattered her breast in the moonlight and warned him—with

her death.

VIII

He turned; he spurred to the West; he did not know who stood
    Bowed, with her head o'er the musket, drenched with her own red blood!
    Not till the dawn he heard it, his face grew grey to hear
    How Bess, the landlord's daughter,
        The landlord's black-eyed daughter,
    Had watched for her love in the moonlight, and died in the darkness there.

IX

Back, he spurred like a madman, shrieking a curse to the sky,
    With the white road smoking behind him and his rapier brandished high!
    Blood-red were his spurs i' the golden noon; wine-red was his velvet coat,
    When they shot him down on the highway,
        Down like a dog on the highway,
    And he lay in his blood on the highway, with the bunch of lace at his throat.

    *   *   *   *   *   *

X

And still of a winter's night, they say, when the wind is in the trees,
    When the moon is a ghostly galleon tossed upon cloudy seas,

When the road is a ribbon of moonlight over the purple moor,
A highwayman comes riding—
      Riding—riding—
A highwayman comes riding, up to the old inn-door.

XI

Over the cobbles he clatters and clangs in the dark inn-yard;
He taps with his whip on the shutters, but all is locked and
barred;
He whistles a tune to the window, and who should be waiting
there
But the landlord's black-eyed daughter,
      Bess, the landlord's daughter,
Plaiting a dark red love-knot into her long black hair.

Example of a silly story poem:

Ted Saves Fred From Being Dead

This is the story of Ted and Fred
One followed his heart and one used his head.
In the Kingdom of Didd, not far from Idd
Where the witches roam with secret Gnomes,
Ted and Fred called that kingdom home.

Everyone in the Kingdom, be they short, be they tall
Everyone was invited to a grand fancy ball!
(Not the kind that bounce, but the kind where you dance.)

Ezmerelda was an evil sorceress, mean and ugly and bad
And she wasn't invited by chance to the dance
and I tell you that made her mad.
She decided to disguise herself as a princess,
and called herself Orchid Bloom
She crashed the castle to find a husband,
and whoever he was, he was doomed.

Ted and his brother Fred were dancing
with all the ladies in the grand Kingdom Hall.
When suddenly, Fred set eyes on Orchid,
the most beautiful princess of all.

Fred said, "What is your name, sweet lady?"
"Sir, you may call me Orchid Bloom."
And Fred danced in a trance under the spell of romance
As he waltzed Orchid all 'cross the room.

It was love at first sight and they danced half the night
Yes, they danced 'til their feet were sore
Fred said, "My Princess, my Queen, I never have seen
someone with feet quite as huge as yours."

She didn't tell him to shove it, she said, "Think nothing of it,
and isn't a lovely night for a carriage ride?"
Would you like to see me home? I live all alone."
Fred said, "I'd be honored to be by your side."

As they were leaving, at that point of the evening,
Ted came up to Fred and he said,
"There could be hitch, I think she might be a witch.
That woman's feet are more huge than my head."

"Fred, you've got to believe me."
"No, she'd never deceive me" And off they rode in her carriage.
There was laughing and drinking and all the time she was thinking,
"How can I fool this fool into marriage?"

Inside Orchid's castle, there was more hugging and kissing
And Fred thought, "poor brother Ted doesn't know what he's missing."

Orchid knew it was now or never
Her magic disguise wouldn't last forever.

"My fine fellow, Fred, what a handsome husband you'll be,

I'm not shy, be my guy, Fred will you please marry me?"

Fred said, "Why I'm so surprised, and I love your eyes,"

And she stepped closer.

"I love your smile, my dear."

And she stepped more near.

"And I love your cute little nose"
And she stepped on his toes.

"But your feet are so huge they would fill up the bed"
And poof! Her disguise disappeared.
And Fred said, "I'm dead"

"That can surely be arranged," she said looking quite strange.
"I could cook you in a stew. Is that what you'd like me to do?
"Better in a stew than married to you," Fred said.

And the witch replied, "Into Alligator Swamp,
I'll throw you from the highest tower.
But if you marry me, I'll be your honey bee
and you, my sweetest flower,"

"I'd rather die a thousand deaths,
Than to have to smell your stinky breath," said Fred with dread.

"Then, down to the dungeon with you!
There's just so much I've got to do.
I'll pour you a bath of soothing oil,
then bring you back here when it starts to boil!"

Then Ezmerelda began to laugh
and Fred said, "It's alright with me if we skip the bath."

She locked him up in her dungeon deep
where skeletons scowl and wild rats sleep.

There in the dark, he saw a pair of scary eyes
and as they came closer, Fred could feel his fear rise.

Closer it came! Higher Fred's fear rose,
until he felt something licking his toes!

Fred said, "It's a black cat I fear. I wish I could see.
I bet it wants to make a meal out of me."

Meanwhile, Fred's brother Ted was approaching the witch's
castle.
He didn't trust that phony princess and knew she'd be a hassle.

He disguised himself as a lion and roared right past the guard.
Then he stole a suit of armor from a soldier in the yard.

He found the witch stirring a boiling pot, and carefully drew
near.
And when she saw him she said, "You're right on time,
Guard, bring the prisoner here."

"And just where might that prisoner be?"
"In the dungeon, you fool, now bring him to me!"

So Ted rescued Fred with his courage and cunning.
And then they snuck out the back door and both took off running.

The witch started to chase them shouting, "I'll have you both in
chains."
When just at that moment it started to rain.

Lucky them, they were saved and justice was dealt.
For witches caught in the rain are destined to melt.

Fred said to Ted, "Ted, I've got to thank you for saving my life.
I wouldn't want to have a witch for a wife."

And Ted said to Fred, "Fred, be careful with the women you meet.
And take my advice, think twice if they've got really big feet."

Rewrites

Take a famous poem and rewrite it in your own words.

If

If you can keep your head when all about you
Are losing theirs and blaming it on you,
If you can trust yourself when all men doubt you
But make allowance for their doubting too,
If you can wait and not be tired by waiting,
Or being lied about, don't deal in lies,
Or being hated, don't give way to hating,
And yet don't look too good, nor talk too wise:

If you can dream--and not make dreams your master,
If you can think--and not make thoughts your aim;
If you can meet with Triumph and Disaster
And treat those two impostors just the same;
If you can bear to hear the truth you've spoken
Twisted by knaves to make a trap for fools,
Or watch the things you gave your life to, broken,
And stoop and build 'em up with worn-out tools:

If you can make one heap of all your winnings
And risk it all on one turn of pitch-and-toss,
And lose, and start again at your beginnings
And never breath a word about your loss;
If you can force your heart and nerve and sinew
To serve your turn long after they are gone,
And so hold on when there is nothing in you
Except the Will which says to them: "Hold on!"

If you can talk with crowds and keep your virtue,
Or walk with kings--nor lose the common touch,
If neither foes nor loving friends can hurt you;
If all men count with you, but none too much,
If you can fill the unforgiving minute
With sixty seconds' worth of distance run,
Yours is the Earth and everything that's in it,
And--which is more--you'll be a Man, my son!

--*Rudyard Kipling*

A New "If"

If you can keep cool when everyone around you
Is stressing out and looking for someone to blame
If you remain confident when no one believes in you
and can forgive them for not being supportive
If you can always be patient about your needs and dreams
without giving up
If you remain honest in all things and never give in to hate

If you realize there is honor in humility
If you hold realistic dreams and think things through
If you're not big headed when you succeed or bitter when you fail
If you don't lash out when people ridicule your ideas
But keep on doing the best you can in the ways you can

If you're not hung up on making money
or acquiring material things
If you have the inner strength to persevere
Even when you're disappointed by what life throws at you
If you realize that everyone has something to offer
whether rich or poor and take time to hear their stories

If you can remember that all the hurtful things people can say about you are
only words
If you can cherish others yet not depend on their love
for your happiness
And if you're glad for each day you're given
And welcome either the sun or the rain
Then the earth and all its joys are yours
And your life will have purpose and meaning
As you create your world.

Grass

By Carl Sandburg

Pile the bodies high at Austerlitz and Waterloo.
Shovel them under and let me work
I am the grass; I cover all

And pile them high at Gettysburg
And pile them high at Ypres and Verdun.
Shovel them under and let me work

Two years, ten years, and the passengers ask the
conductor:
What place is this?
Where are we now?

I am the grass.
Let me work.

New Grass

Bring me the bodies from Nam and Iraq
I will bury deep the pain so it won't come back
I am the earth and death is nothing new to me

Give me every kid that hate and hurt and loss has scarred
And I will sit with them as they heal
Singing nature's songs

I will withstand all the ignorance and folly
Endure your pollution and your politics
Every sad thing you bring

I am from whence you are created
The breath of life
And I will live on long after you're gone

I am the earth
Let me work

Two roads diverged in a yellow wood,
And sorry I could not travel both
And be one traveler, long I stood
And looked down one as far as I could
To where it bent in the undergrowth;

Then took the other, as just as fair,
And having perhaps the better claim
Because it was grassy and wanted wear,
Though as for that the passing there
Had worn them really about the same,

And both that morning equally lay
In leaves no step had trodden black.
Oh, I marked the first for another day!
Yet knowing how way leads on to way
I doubted if I should ever come back.

I shall be telling this with a sigh
Somewhere ages and ages hence:
Two roads diverged in a wood, and I,
I took the one less traveled by,
And that has made all the difference.

Robert Frost

New Two Roads or "Winds of Change"

With the winds what they are
And no sight of stars
You could sail either up wind or down

If you've no place to go
Don't mind where the wind blows
Getting somewhere or just getting around

For who's the more free?
Those on land or on sea?
If freedom is just freeing the mind?

Is it those under sail?
Or those who sit there and wail?
Let's not weep for the ones left behind.

Poem

I loved my friend
He went away from me
There's nothing more to say
The poem ends
Soft as it began
I loved my friend

By Langston Hughes

A New Poem

I loved you so

Didn't think you'd go

Don't really understand what it means.

But when love goes

Steps on your toes

It's still pain in the moments between.

Imagery (Tell It In Pictures Poetry):

You can read poems silently, but it's better to hear them. Even so, it's not just an auditory experience; it's the pictures a poem can create in your head that help to bring it alive. Have the students write focusing on a visual image.

Garden Variety Poem

Stair
Stepped
Stoned
Garden
Brook became
A bathtub for birds
Flutter feathered friends
In frolicking play on an afternoon day
                  Of sun and cloud

Water
Wings
Wonder filled I
                  Overflowed
                      Into the image of
                        This pool/poem

Mood

Have the students pick a mood from the following list and write a poem, free verse or rhyming that expresses that mood. Make it clear that the mood need not be the topic of the poem.

Afraid, Annoyed, Apathetic, Alarmed, Ashamed, Angry, Anxious, Bashful, Brave, Bored, Bewildered, Calm, Curious,

Confused, Confident, Crushed, Desperate, Doubtful, Defeated, Disgusted, Depressed, Disliked, Dejected, Disappointed,

Discouraged, Disturbed, Eager, Envious, Exhausted, Embarrassed, Frustrated, Frantic, Fed Up, Furious, Frightened,

Grateful, Guilty, Gloomy, Grieving, Grouchy, Happy, Hopeless, Humiliated, Horrified, Hurt, Helpless, Hopeful, Humble,

Impatient, Infatuated, Irritated, Indifferent, Insecure, Insulted, Jealous, Jittery, Lazy, Lost, Loved, Lonely, Mad, Mischievous,

Miserable, Nervous, Nosey, Optimistic, Overwhelmed, Peaceful, Panicked, Pressured, Puzzled, Proud, Pessimistic,

Patient, Rejected, Relieved, Regretful, Stubborn, Suspicious, Shocked, Shy, Surprised, Troubled, Thrilled, Trusting, Tense,

Trapped, Tempted, Uncomfortable, Used, Unwanted, Unhappy, Upset, Worried, Worthless

Apathy

Apathy stings the air
And I don't care
I don't care at all

I've grown weary of striving
I'm tired of trying to set things straight

I've lost interest in causes
And glorious revolution

Instead of pointing out problems
           I search for solutions
And fail all too often

People preach the brotherhood of man
      but can't swallow their pride
           It's no wonder it builds up inside
                To blow sky high
      Between heaven and hell
                But, oh well
                Woe is me

                It seems I've grown tired

                      of apathy

Personification Poems

These poems give human characteristics to inanimate objects:

<u>Example:</u>

<u>Flashy Thing</u>

She has a photographic memory

you can take her anywhere

she is flashy but stylish

if you're not careful, you will lose her

if you don't treat her well, she will have a break down

she won't help you to see things in a different light.

she is picture perfect

you can see right through her

she likes to be held close to your face

she takes her time

this darling camera of mine

<u>Shoe Talk</u>   by Shel Silverstein

There's no one to talk with

    I'll talk with my shoe

He does have a tongue

    And an inner soul, too

He's awfully well polished

    So straight laced and neat

But he talks about nothing

        but feet, feet, feet.

Blender Mind Bender

She makes the best drinks

When you press her button she roars

She loves to eat food

She works in your kitchen

When she's by water you can see sparks

Sometimes she's a hazard

You have to make sure her mouth's closed tight or

She'll throw up in your face

Sometimes she smoking hot

You can see what's going on in the inside

She makes loud weird noises

Poetic Devices, Lessons and Activities

<u>Rhyme:</u> Same vowel sound. (pray, grey)
Ask the students to come up with five rhymes for the following vowel sounds or words:
Day   (play, say, neigh, prey, hey)
Hat   (Splat, flat, gnat, that, Pat)
Free   (Sea, pea, knee, glee, be)
Fred   (Sled, red, head, fed, lead)
Die   (Sigh, shy, pie, guy, rye)
Dig   (dig, rig, fig, wig, big)
Slow   (Flow, show, tow, grow, bow)
Grew   (few, too, blue, who, you)
Rug   (tug, slug, bug, jug, hug)

Notice that there are many combinations of vowels that rhyme even though they don't have the same spelling such as You and Flew.

<u>Rhyming poem example:</u>

<u>Rain On My Brain</u>

Rain, rain on my brain
We came to school
We must be insane
The roads are flooding
The streams are high
But we came to school
We don't know why
So here we sit
We're soaking wet
And as freezing cold as you can get
No one's learning
It's quite a mess
At least there'll be no algebra test
We've got puddles everywhere
Dripping clothes and frizzled hair
Please close this school
And we'll go home
At least we wrote
This rainy poem

<u>Rhythm</u>: The beat to the lines, like how a drum beat accentuates music.

<u>Alliteration</u>: A sentence with two or three words that start with the same sound.
Note: I usually don't teach alliteration and assonance on the same day. Kids tend to mix up the two. I demonstrate a few sentences, then have the class create a few with me, listing them on the board or overhead, and finally ask them to come up with five sentences showing alliteration.

Examples: I found a few fantastic phones.
The wind went whipping through our classroom.
My mom is mean to men.

<u>Assonance</u>: A sentence with two or three words that have the same vowel sound (rhyme) Again, model, do some together, then ask the kids to write five examples.

Examples: Why is it shy guys rarely lie?
You have to pay to play in the game today.
Ted said the sled hit his head.

Rhyme Scheme: The rhyme pattern

Example: AAA, BB, CC, DD

A poetry time

    Is playing with rhyme

        Bouncing ideas off your mind

Like a juggling ball, That's all

It's a time to reflect and fly

        To wonder "Why?"

And thank you for being a part

        Bless your heart

Two examples of different rhyme schemes:

A   I'm a hopeless teenager
B   But I'll make it somehow
C   Life is for living
B   And I'm going to live mine now

A   Poor little mosquito
B   He has drawn his last breath
C   For he
C   Who bites me
B   Tastes death

Simile: Comparison using the words "like" or "as".
Examples: She can run like the wind.
He's as trustworthy as a fox in a hen house.
He can swear like a pirate when he's angry.

Metaphor: A poetic comparison.

Examples: She is the sunlight in my day.
You are a breath of fresh air in this class.

History is the bridge to our past.

<u>Onomatopoeia</u>: sound effect words or words that sound like the action they describe.

<u>Examples</u>:
The ball <u>crashed</u> through the window.
The book hit the floor with a <u>thud</u>.
Without warning, <u>bam</u>, the guy hits me from the side.

<u>Meter</u>: the rhythm pattern of lines in a poem. The arrangement of the accented words, or syllables, in a line of poetry.

Roses are Dead

Roses are red, violets are blue
Seriously now, is this the best you can do?

I don't want corny clichés
Or recycled rhymes

I want good times
Fun talks
Quiet walks

Don't declare your love for me
  with someone else's poetry

I want to hear your heart speak
  Make me weak in the knees
    But please
No worn out phrases
  I need longing gazes
    Your eyes and your touch
    Say so much

Stanza: a group of lines of poetry arranged in a specific order. A verse of a poem. (See" The Highwayman" earlier in this book)

Free Verse: poems that can have internal rhyme or no rhyme at all. It breaks all the rules. The words can be arranged in any way on the page.

For example:

Shout This Poem

I travel at the speed of poetry

       Moving though time

Free

       To rhyme of ramble

I roam about

    I sing this poem

      I laugh

        I shout this poem to the stars

Such sweet release

      A poem for peace

       In this world of ours.

Poetic Devices Test

Match the following terms with their definition: Rhyme Scheme, Simile, Rhythm, Assonance, Rhyme, Alliteration.

1. _____: Words that have the same vowel sound (reign, pain).

2. _____: The beat to the lines of poetry.

3. _____: A sentence with two or three words that start with the same sound. (ex. My mom gets so mad at me).

4. _____: The rhyme pattern.

5. _____: Comparison using the words "like" or "as". (ex. You're pretty <u>as</u> a summer's day.)

6. _____: A sentence with two or three words that have the same vowel sound. (rhyme) (ex. If I do the crime I'm doing the time)

True or False

7. T or F   "She is the sunlight in my day" is a metaphor.

8. T or F "She is as beautiful as a summer's day" is not a simile.

9. T or F "The Wind went whipping through Waikiki" is an example of "Assonance".

10. T or F "We took the brown cow to town" is an example of "Alliteration".

11. T or F "I was born to be bad" is an example of Alliteration.

12. T or F "To be happy, pray and play several times a day" is an example of "Assonance".

Question 13:   If it starts to snow
                   On the mountain top
                   We'll eat cookie dough
                   Until we pop.

The "Rhyme Scheme" for the poem above is:

 1) ABBA 2) ABC 3) AABB 4) ABAB

Comparing Poems

Pick any two poems and have at it. You might want to compare the "Jaberwocky" to "The Vorpal Snit" (earlier in this book). Or find the darkness in Poe's "The Raven" and then look for similar images from the Twilight movies and books.

I prefer writing poems rather than just talking about them and that may be true of your students. Though, having been a teacher, I realize modeling the art of comparison can sometimes be a requirement.

Example: comparing the follow two flutter-by poems.

I wish I was a butterfly

    And if you ever ask me "Why?"

I'd say, "I want to flutter by,

        To fly on loving wings."

A Flutter-by in frolic flight

If wish you may,

Then wish you might

For peace on earth
A peace so dear

Now look around.

It's here.

It's here!

Comparing "I Wish" with "Flutter-by"

What do they have in common? Butterflies.
Imagining/wishing.

Any phrases in common? Flutter by/flutter-by and
fly/flight.

Any themes or messages in common? The joy of flying
in the first and a realization of a peaceful moment in the
second.

Any other observations? Both poems are short and use
simple language. The first one uses the butterfly/flutter
by play on words and the second uses flutter-by as
another word for butterfly.

An example of comparing two poems about war:

"Teddy Boy"

Teddy walked off to war

          And cried

He killed a man

     And cried

And Teddy the boy died

Ted the man lived on

    With patriotism to hide his shame

    And war's lethal legalities

       to clear his name.

"Betty Sue"

Betty Sue of Tuscaloo
        walks along the railroad tracks
                that pass through her small town

Looking down and remembering the young man, Dan
        who passed through her life
                                her town
                                        her love

He came to build a school
        He left to fight a war a world away

And when came the day
        that train brought him back
                as he stood there beside the track
                        Betty Sue instinctively knew
                                that the love she once had come to know
                        had died in a battle not so long ago

And only a body here remained
        to carry around the living pain
like the lonesome moan of a passing train

Comparing "Teddy Boy" and "Betty Sue"

1) What they have in common:

Both suggest that the experience of war can hurt a soldier deeply: Teddy is wracked with shame and Dan is hollow or dead inside. Both characters are young men who survived a war. They both convey a sense of sadness. They're both poems that tell a story and stress a point of view. They're both rhyming poems.

2) How they're different:

Teddy is the star of his poem but Dan shares the poem equally with Betty Sue. Teddy is shorter, less detailed. Betty Sue is about both heartache and the pain of war.

Fieldtrips For Poets

Organize a fieldtrip for you students to an interesting place to write about. They can create movement poems by looking out the window as the bus takes them where they're going. Fun places to write about might be: the zoo, a museum, a play or concert, a haunted house, a walk along a river, a hike, an architectural tour, or the beach (if you have one nearby).

That Boring Zoo

I went with my stupid class
To a boring zoo
With lazy elephants
And hopeless hopping kangaroos
The monkeys seemed as bored as me
And I'm embarrassed to tell you about the chimpanzees
The alligators just looked like logs
They even had a home for frogs
There were condors and eagles and cockatoos
And my favorite was the petting zoo
I heard the songs of peacocks, flamingos, loons
I hope we can go back there soon

Poem a day (an assignment in verse):

Write a poem a day.

Have fun.

"when is it done?"

whenever you're through

"how will I know?"

that's up to you

"where will it lead?"

where do you think?

"Why should I care?"

If you can't, the poem stinks.

Being "Concise" would be nice.

Keeping it short when there's so much to say

is being concise

words don't get in the way

poems from the heart

poems for the head

keeping this brief

still, so much gets said.

How we gonna find something new

if'n we don't write it and give it a view?

Read it to a friend or two

A poem a day to capture your thoughts

the what what's

and why's

the "what I'm thinkings"

and sprinklings of inspiration

rhythm nation

poetic confrontation situation

It's just a poem a day

Try to get carried away.

For Days (or was it four?)

Directions: Write one short poem each day for four days and turn them in all together on a Friday. They don't have to rhyme. They can be about whatever you like. You are required to have fun doing this assignment or you're not doing it right.

The Loving Thing

Concise

is nice

my advice

is look for the loving thing

to say or do

and that will say

a lot

about you

Being a poet

means you don't have to wait

just anywhere wondering

what to do or think

to pass the time

You can rhyme

Or free verse

Rehearse your thoughts on paper

Or capture a breathless moment

of irreverent rejoicing

emotions and questions and hopes and dreams

revelations

situations

if you do it

you can't do it wrong

A Metaphor Lesson Plan

1)   Explain to your students that a metaphor is a comparison used often in poetry to give deeper meaning and clarification to a poet's ideas, images and themes.

Example: the metaphor in Robert Frost's poem about two roads diverging in the wood: the road is a metaphor for life's journey and the decisions we make. Quote: "Two roads diverged in the wood, and I, I took the one less traveled by, and that has made all the difference."

2) Ask the students what the following metaphors could mean: He's a mountain (big and solid). She's a flower (delicate and beautiful). Life's a party (a place for fun). Iraq's a graveyard (a place with many dead people).

3)   Read to the students Whitman's, ", My Captain!" explaining that the metaphor of a ship's captain was used to describe Abraham Lincoln.   Then read them the following example of a poem with an extended metaphor:

Life is a Road

Life is a road with many different paths to choose from.

It has its ups and downs

You must go at your own speed and there is often something in your way:

Stoplights are telling you to stop and look at things from a different perspective

SUV obstacles and Traffic Jams are dreams delayed.

The back roads can be pathways to new opportunities or sidetracking trouble like drugs or crime

Oh, yes, Life's road has many twists and turns

One big curve is marriage (talk about changing lanes!)

Detours are when you're sick or injured.

Intersections are decisions.

If there are bumps in the road, don't let them stop you

Pay attention to where you're going

Don't get distracted like someone talking on their cell phone while driving

And keep in mind, in the end, we all have to exit.

4) Have your students write the line and then chose one of the options to fill in the blank.

My country 'tis a ship,
Sailing on _____
(global seas, troubled waters, oily seas, stormy seas, waves of terror)
Crewed by _____
(people from all nations, people of diversity, you and me)
Bourne on the winds of _____
(freedom, change, war)
Kept afloat by _____
(military might, our hopes and dreams, inflated dollars)
Seeking safe harbor_____
(in a place of peace, in the constitution, in freedom's future)
On this journey to_____
(freedom's shore, our future, our nation's destiny)

For more advanced work, the students should fill in the blanks with their own words and phrases.

5) Read the following poem with its "crossroads" metaphor and discuss how life is shaped by the decisions we make.

The Crossroads

Welcome to the crossroads, kid
The start and end of everything
You ever did
Here, decisions run in different directions
That way or this
Depression or bliss
What road you on, kid?
Slip, slide or skid
Dash, crash or cruise
Life lets you choose
Dreamer or schemer
Grouch, slouch, or couch potato
Which way you gonna go?
Fast, slow, high, low
Or just sit and sing the blues
You gotta choose
Blues can be a reason to sing
Isn't it all just how you look at a thing?

6) Have the students pick one of the following suggested metaphors and write an extended metaphor poem, story, or essay. They should make as many comparisons as they can, keeping within the framework of the initial metaphor they choose.

Life as a road

School as a video game

Earth as a mother

Television as a teacher

Your brain as a computer

Learning as a car ride

War as a chicken fight

Love as a sport

Your school as a food

Romance as a computer program

7) End the unit by reading aloud the students poems. They may read their own, or read each others' writing, or the teacher may read the students compositions.

The teacher may also read one of the following examples or one of his or her own:

 Poetic Metaphor example:

> <u>Over-population is a disease</u>

Over time
    Over population
        In every town, place and nation
    Our planet has a virus
        And it's us
Fast-spreading and deadly
    With weapons of disease
           Concrete and
              Huge numbers

More all the time
    More than ever before
        How many more will it take
Till earth breaks
    Gives in
        Gives out

Poor little planet with a bad case

        Of humanity

Let love grow

Love is a flower

So let it bloom

Plant the seed

And give it room

Believe in the flower

Without any doubt

Water it daily

And watch it sprout

Be gentle and patient

And take it slow

And you will see how beautiful

Love will grow

Alliteration Assignment:

Alliteration is when several words that begin with the same sound, appear in the same sentence.

Examples:

(3 w's) The wind went whipping through the classroom.

(4 sh's)Sheena shouldn't shout at Sherry.

(5 p's)Peter Paniola picked pilau papaya

(22 t's) I've just got To Tell you, Today Tim Told Todd To Tell Tina Tons of Tall Tales about Texas Tea and Tennesse Toadstools and the Two Towns: Talahasee and Tampa with their Terrible Tornados.

Write at least five sentences with different alliteration sounds. For advanced work, write a poem as well, using alliteration more than once.

<u>Assonance:</u> When a sentence has three or more words that have the same vowel sound. In other words, three words that rhyme.

<u>Examples of Assonance:</u>

I am free to be just me.

Please don't sneeze on these cupcakes.

I just want to say it's OK to play.

I play guitar like a superstar in my fancy car.

I try to convince my brain that with exercise, it's no pain, no gain.

Mrs. Norris stood before us to implore us to work harder

To throw snow is a chilling blow.

He threw a snit fit and hit me.

My fat cat played with a rat.

She thinks she's cool but fell in the pool, the fool.

The lead hit Ted in the head, now he's dead.

The living dead, with eyes so red, caught Fred and fed or so they said.

It made me cry when the fly flew in my eye

Let's play down by bay today

I go with the flow on the down low

Matt was so fat he squished my hat

From the start you've held my heart but now it's broken all apart.

Why are you so shy, little guy?

I think the sink stinks.

Give Stan a hand, man.

She won't pass the muster if you can't trust her, Buster.

Soap slime will remove the grime in time.

You can cope and have hope if you avoid dope.

Ted's red sled is in Fred's shed.

Was it you who threw the shoe?

Onomatopoeia Assignment

Write a poem or story using words with "Onomatopoeia." Those are words that sound like the action they describe. HINT: Write about places that are noisy with a variety of sounds such as a factory, concert, TV show, department store, big city, subway train, parade, sporting event, war zone, Star Wars battle, water park, cafeteria, beach, movie, video arcade, bowling alley, spaceship, submarine, carnival, concert, or prison.

How many of the following words can you use in a poem or story featuring sounds?

Flick, crack, whack, sniff, rumble, grrr, poof, quack,

Tick tock, bam, ding dong, sniffle, kaboom, meow,

moo, tinkle, swoosh, smack, scratch, vroom, crunch,

boing, slam, poke, chirp, ha ha, caw, rustle, swish,

snap, putput, scrape, chuckle, clip, clop, ring, clank,

hachoo, crackle, splash, zip, boink, creek, ho ho ho,

burp, boom, pop, splat, slurp, bang, thump, gush, rip,

screech, crash, woosh, thud, bong, clink, mash, oink,

scrunch, cockadoodledoo, clang, zap, slash, kaching

flap, slap, tap, honk, blast, squeak, tweet, beep, clap.

Can you list any other "sound words?

_____

_____

_____

Two Examples of Onomatopoeia Poetry:

Meow my fine cats
Arf arf all you dogs
Cheep Cheep you little chickies
Nee Deep my friendly frogs

Moo to you cows
Neigh you young colts
Whack whack darling ducks
You be Baaaad you old goats

Camping Sounds

Boulders rumble as they roll down the shore towards the sea until...swoosh, the waves bring them back, scraping them against each other like thunder! I set down my pack with a thud, grab my canteen and slurp...ah, swallow a cool gulp. Suddenly, whoosh, the wind picks up and...rip, part of the tarp over my hammock tears. I drop the camp pots onto the campfire grill with a bang and go retie my tarp. The trees creak as branches rub against each other. It's time to cook dinner before the dark sets in and I can't see to eat.

Simile Test:

Complete the following comparisons:

Hot (as or like)

Hungry (as or like)

Smart (as or like)

Dumb (as or like)

Beautiful (as or like)

Tall (as or like)

Small (as or like)

Hard (as or like)

Cold (as or like)

Cute (as or like)

Fast (as or like)

Boring (as or like)

Tough (as or like)

New (as or like)

Rough (as or like)

Peaceful (as or like)

Big (as or like)

Thrilling (as or like)

Fun (as or like)

Bright (as or like)

Sweet (as or like)

Black (as or like)

Scary (as or like)

Stinks (as or like)

Graceful (as or like)

Rich (as or like)

Cool (as or like)

Strange (as or like)

Slow (as or like)

Sharp (as or like)

Loud (as or like)

Evil (as or like)

Slow (as or like)

Strong (as or like)

Underline or Circle the Similes in these two poems:

Love
Like butterflies in my tummy
Stirs me up like a milkshake

Your eyes shining like stars
In the night
I need no other light

When you're near
My heart beats fast as raindrops on the roof

I'm drawn to you
Like a moth to a flame

Speak my name
And I am awestruck
Such good luck to know you
And I want to know you completely
Like I know my family

Lock Up

School is like a prison

Everyone waits in line for the food

Fighting is not allowed

on the playground or in the pen

Our ID's are like the prisoner's numbers

Our uniform compares to their orange jumpsuit

We have weight training, they have the rec area

Suspension is like being put in solitary confinement

Graduation is like parole

and in the end, the question is always the same:

Have you learned your lesson?

Or are you coming back?

Revising

Reread the poem several times.

Have someone else read it aloud to you and make comments on it.

Is there anything that can be shortened or left out that won't change the meaning or messages of the poem? This will help it to be more concise (less wordy).

Is there something you can add to help clarify the points you're trying to make?

Could you change some of the words to find a word that is clearer or more expressive?

Are there any parts that sound awkward that perhaps could be rearranged or reworked?

What are the most memorable parts of the poem and could it benefit from repeating them or restating them again in some other words?

Is there anything that sounds corny or dumb or lame that should be cut out or reworked?

Does the poem effect our feelings?

Are there any specific images in the poem or could it use more?

How does the rhythm of the lines feel?

Were there any surprises? Should there be?

When someone else reads it, what do they remember most?

Could punctuation or the arrangement of the words on the page strengthen the clarity of the poem?

Is there any part of the poem that's confusing that you could make clearer?

What Is Truth?

The truth shall set you free
  Let's see. Let's see.

What is truth?

Can anyone give us just the facts?
The world is flat or so folks once did say
Surely they have passed away
  And with them their eternal truths
     So oft abuse
    Or lost amid confusion

If truth is being right
  From which perspective shall we look
    And not be blinded by biased light

And if the word "Truth" were carved in stone
  Mountain high and in a line

   Remember stone still turns to dust

   Amid the test of time.

Truth Revised

What is truth?

Who's to say?

Can truth, like man, pass away?

If the word were carved in stone

Mountain Big and in a line

Doesn't stone wear down to dust

amid the test of time?

The following is a lengthy poem, followed by the revised shorter version.

I sit in this room
And write this poem
Don't exist
I am a tree that fell in some forest
        And no one heard the sound
Don't exist
I am a frightened young man
        Wanting to know what love is
            No one can tell me
Does love exist?
I feel, taste, touch, see, hurt, but don't cry
            Though I wish I would
Don't exist
I'm lost, lonely, hungry, sad
And no one heard this tree fall
Don't exist
        And no one heard
Don't exist
        No one

I am a tree standing in this forest
        With only cold wind in the branches
                            To cry out
        My words are misshapen
                        Misunderstood
                Even if someone would hear
        No one

Don't exist
I'm falling in a forest
More wind through branches
       Louder cry,
            "I exist!"

                  No one

through the wind
in my forest
near the ground
breaking branches
pounding
broken hopes
resounding in my room
         my forest
     no one heard
   don't exist

don't write this poem: exist.

Alone in my room
    On no one's mind
Don't exist
    On pieces of paper
        In banks
          On lists
           In files
                  Exist
     Pieces of paper exist

Writing a poem

                  Poem exists

Should I leave this room

                Touch someone

                  See someone

                    Be heard

                            Exist

Change my world

        This world

            For good or bad

            But

          Good and bad don't exist

In ethics books

    On dusty shelves

    Waiting for someone seeking some answer

                    Some reason

           Some justification for being

Good and bad

    In black ink

        On off-white paper

                  Exists

    Pieces of paper exist

Pieces of paper with my name on it

             My name exists

A tree fell in a forest

    No one heard the sound

      I don't care

            Tree exists

Still in my room

        Writing this poem

   On no one's mind
I don't care
      I exist
A word called caring
     On a piece of paper
       Abstract concept
        Paper exists

I don't care
I do care
I exist
No one heard
I exist
No one cares
I exist
Someone cares
I hope

The revision

Alone in my head
   On no one's mind
Do I exist?

   My name
     On pieces of paper

          In files, on lists, exists
Pieces of paper exist

Writing this poem
    Black ink on off-white paper
        Poem exists

I'm a tree falling in a forest
    (trees fall to become paper)
        with no one to hear the sound
I don't care
    This tree exists

        Alone in this forest
            This room
                My head
          Writing this poem
               On no one's mind
I don't care, I exist
    A word called caring
        Written in black ink
Though writing doesn't make it so

I don't care
I do care
I exist
Even if no one hears, I exist
Even if no one cares, I exist
Someone, someday, will care, I hope.

Another example of Revision:

Why write?
    Pressed to write
    Stressed, uptight
    Impressed? Alright

Who'd have guessed I might compose
                Words so free of prose?

Images that stand, though leaning
    In need of the support of meaning

Semantic flippery
    Catch my slippery drift?

      I am adrift in a sea of words

Gulping down mouthfuls of metaphor
    Washed up on the
        "someone's already done this" shore

Hang this poem
      Up to dry
          And remember
            Never ever
               Ask a poet, "Why?"

<u>Here's the same poem edited to be more concise:</u>

Why?

Why write?

Why bother to compose
   poetry and prose?

 Hasn't somebody said it all before?

   How can there be more to say?

   And who would listen, anyway?

Might as well hang this poem up to dry

 And never ask a poet, "Why?"

Have the cuts hurt or helped this poem?

The answer is in the ear of the beholder.

Getting Feedback

When students hear a poem read to them, or read one silently to themselves, there are many questions they can answer to show how well they understand the poem:

Did the poem deal with any emotions or feelings, and if so, describe them?

What is the over-all message of this this poem?

What visual images (pictures in your mind) came to you from this poem?

Did you notice any other sense images such as taste, touch, smell or sounds? If so, what were they?

What is the over-all mood of this poem? (Happy, sad, scary, hopeful, angry, silly, etc)

If the poem is about a person, describe them.

What do you think is the best line or phrase in the poem and why?

If this poem were going to be made into a video, what camera shots would you suggest?

What Poetic Devices did this poem have? (rhyme, rhythm, simile, metaphor, alliteration, assonance, repetition)

Were there any words in the poem that are new to you?

How would you describe this poem to one of your friends?

Some kids like it quiet. They don't want anyone to overhear them getting feedback on their writing. One way to handle this is "The Silent Approach." It's done with partners:

<u>Poetry Partners Feedback:</u> exchange poems with your partner and read your partner's poem silently to yourself. Each of you may then quietly ask your partner just one question about the poem.

Now write your answers for the following feedback questions:

What was your first reaction to the poem?

What question did you ask to learn more about the poem?

What images came to mind when reading the poem?

What message is the poet trying to tell you through this poem?

What is your favorite phrase (or part) of the poem?

Finding the messages in poems

What is the author's message in the following poem?

Alone in my head
  On no one's mind
Do I exist?

  My name
    On pieces of paper
      In files, on lists, exists
Pieces of paper exist

Writing this poem
  Black ink on off-white paper
    Poem exists
I'm a tree falling in a forest
  (trees fall to become paper)
    with no one to hear the sound
I don't care
  This tree exists

    Alone in this forest
      This room
        My head
     Writing this poem
       On no one's mind
I don't care: I exist
  A word called caring
    Written in black ink
Though writing doesn't make it so

I don't care
I do care
I exist
Even if no one hears, I exist
Even if no one cares, I exist
Someone, someday, will care, I hope.

In the following poem, is the guy alive or dead and what's author's message?

Betty Sue of Tuskaloo
Walks along the railroad tracks
That pass through her small town

Looking down and remembering the young man, Dan
Who passed through her life
                    Her town
                    Her love

He came to build a school
He left to fight a war a world away

And when came the day
That train brought him back
As he stood there beside the track
Betty Sue instinctively knew
That the love she once had come to know
Had died in a battle not so long ago

And only a body here remained
To carry around the living pain
Like the lonesome moan of a passing train

Poetry Portfolios

From the start of your poetry unit (or experiences spread out throughout the year) it's a good idea to encourage your students to keep a Poetry Portfolio or collection of their poems (and other forms of writing). This can be graded periodically or as a final grade and can be used for class presentations or family night showcases. You can encourage the kids to comment on what they've written, and occasionally require that they revise some of their work to improve it.

Some things the portfolio may contain: table of contents, class assigned poems, commentary on the meaning of the poems by the student/author, extra credit poems, tests on poetic devices and feedback on student work and professional poets.

Literary Magazines

Each quarter, I would schedule time in our schools computer lab so the students could type up their best work (poems or stories) to be compiled in a Literary Magazine to be put on display in our school library, Curriculum Fairs and Parents Night or Open House. Usually, there were several students with artistic ability who were willing to submit artwork for the cover or to be included throughout the magazine. You can divide the book into sections by each class, each with it's own table of contents, so parents and friends can find specific works.

When it comes to deciding which poems to include in the collection I suggest each student is permitted from one to three poems, then groups of students can be put in charge of selecting the best in certain categories such as "Best Personification Poem" or "Best Free Verse" etc. You can even have awards for the Gold, Silver and Bronze of the Magazine. I'm not big on competitiveness when it comes to poetry, but some students thrive on it. And finally, the teacher should reserve the right to censor or delete any poem deemed inappropriate (it happens).

There's also the issue of proof reading the manuscript. The teacher had better check every submission lest something come back to "bite you." Also, you have to decide whether to correct all spelling and grammar. It's fine if you have time and it's wonderful when you have help from others. This is why I ask the kids to type things up on computer and <u>save everything</u> in case changes need to be made.

Some Famous Poems and Poets

Eve Merriam: "How to Eat a Poem"

Robert Frost: "Two Roads"

Emily Dickinson "Because I Could Not Stop For Death"

Shel Silverstein: "Shoe Talk" (personification) "Hug of War" (rhyme and theme)

Carl Sandburg: "Grass" (theme)

Lewis Carroll: "Jaberwocky" (nonsense words)

Ogden Nash: "The Germ" "Spring Song"

The Germ
A mighty creature is the germ,
Though smaller than the pachyderm.
His customary dwelling place
Is deep within the human race.
His childish pride he often pleases
By giving people strange diseases.
Do you, my poppet, feel infirm?
You probably contain a germ.

Laura Richards: "Eletelephony"

Once there was an elephant,
Who tried to use the telephant-
No! No! I mean an elephone
Who tried to use the telephone-
(Dear me! I am not certain quite
That even now I've got it right.)

Howe'er it was, he got his trunk
Entangled in the telephunk;
The more he tried to get it free,
The louder buzzed the telephee-
(I fear I'd better drop the song
Of elephop and telephong!)

Foul Shot by Edwin A. Hoey

With two 60s stuck on the scoreboard
And two seconds hanging on the clock,
The solemn boy in the center of eyes,
Squeezed by silence,
Seeks out the line with his feet,
Soothes his hands along his uniform,
Gently drums the ball against the floor,

Then measures the waiting net,
Raises the ball on his right hand,
Balances it with his left,
Calms it with fingertips,
Breathes,
Crouches,
Waits,
And then through a stretching of stillness,
Nudges it upward.

The ball
Slides up and out,
Lands,
Leans,
Wobbles,
Wavers,
Hesitates,
Exasperates,
Plays it coy
Until every face begs with unsounding screams—
And then
And then
And then,
Right before ROAR-UP,
Dives down and through.

Langston Hughes: "Harlem"

What happens to a dream deferred?

Does it dry up
like a raisin in the sun?
Or fester like a sore—
And then run?
Does it stink like rotten meat?
Or crust and sugar over—
like a syrupy sweet?

Maybe it just sags
like a heavy load.

Or does it explode?

<u>Two poems for you teachers:</u>

One of my sources for this book is a poetry unit I put together while attending the College of Education at the University of Hawaii, Manoa (valley of rainbows). I created that unit for three reasons: I'd get credit for it, I liked writing poetry, and I thought I could use it in my student teaching. It has served me well and I've expanded on it over the twenty-two years I've been a teacher. In looking through that unit, I found tucked away in the back, a free verse writing assignment on the topic "Motives and Emerging Concepts."

<u>Time and Attentions</u>

I would like to set kids free

    Of fears on inadequacy

To base my teaching space

      On invitations and expectations

Asking those I teach for creativity

And new ideas

Because I believe for this old world

To keep from blowing itself sky high

We had better give some new ideas a try

I want my class room to be a place of potential

And life-long learning

Not having all the answers

But learning where answers can be found

I would let them know they're loved

By giving my time and attention

Hoping that by example

they would see how essential is love

I want to encourage inquisitive thinking

Inner awareness

Confident self-concepts

Whole humans

I want my students to write

    If not well, then often

(and 'well' will take care of itself)

To speak loud and clear

So someday the whole world can hear

I'd rather not tell them what they must do

But guide them to what they are capable of doing

To offer choices

To value their creative suggestions

Disapproving of anyone trying to get out of work

Yet approving of getting at the work in different ways

I want to be a guide, not a guard

    Not a disciplinarian but a humanitarian

Hoping my students will learn

To treat me and each other as they would like to be treated

Only that one real rule… and it's golden

Teaching Up A Storm

I'm a teacher

and I enjoy teaching kids to question

to dream

and what it means to be a life-long learner.

And I hope to get to it, when I get a chance…

Once attendance is taken

the rules reviewed

passes handed out

grade checks signed

kids excused to counseling and student government and dentist

and doctor appointments.

After we've collected for the fundraiser

and I've paid the kids for cookies and car washes

signed their fieldtrip forms

listed the day's date and events

handed out tissues and band aids

pencils and pens

and provided the impoverished with paper products.

There's so much I have to share with the kids

when I'm done with all my meetings and workshops

Just as soon as I implement all those top-down requirements

Posted the posters and benchmarks and standards

finished the paperwork

integrate the interdisciplinary lessons

read and replied to the e-mails

I intend to do some serious teaching

after I clean their desk tops

repair broken books and fans

Pick up their discarded papers, broken pens and chewed pencils

I want to find new and exciting stories, ideas,

And issues to hold their interest

And I'll organize some fieldtrips

as I keep parents, and team members and administration

continually appraised of each child's progress and potential

Once we've translated, integrated and appreciated

all appropriate standards…

When all their giggles and whispers and gossip have quieted

and all extraneous questions have been answered…

After I've checked their planners

read them the bulletin

Just as soon as I pick up all their candy wrappers

counsel away their tears and fears

approved all bathroom breaks and quick drinks

having monitored their appearance and attire

calmed the hyper

awakened the sleepy

caught the gum chewers

encouraged the reluctant

protected the innocent

locked out the late comers

As soon as I figure out a way to

corner their two minute attention spans

Having confiscated their laser pointers, I-pods, earphones,

rubber bands, spit balls, paper airplanes and cell phones.

Celebrated their birthdays with well wishes

Distributed all the thrilling test prep materials

Just as soon as I can create a lesson plan to help the kids

suffering from abuse and neglect

lack of respect

heartbreak and headache

After I've given special attention to every disability

To avoid lawsuit liability

Just as soon as I get organized

and finish my professional development

plan the next necessary sabbatical

Prepare for official evaluations

patrol my area

gobble down lunch

run off the materials I need

laminate the goals and remember those reminders

I plan to teach up a storm

as soon as I get back to my class

after the false alarms and shelters in place

and lock downs, earthquake drills, and campus evacuations

After I coordinate with colleagues

teach to the tests

fill out deficiency forms

file all referrals

answer all e-mails

grade all assessments

I will declare what's appropriate, moral and good

(though not necessarily true)

as I adhere to ever changing policies and programs

in an ever changing world

just as soon as I get the hang of the schedule and calendar options

leaving no child behind

figure out any report card changes

And I plan to do so, controlling the kids

without touching, threatening, or harassing them

Without losing my temper or my sanity.

As each day, I forgive their homework forgotten or misplaced

stashed in gym lockers or someone else's class

eaten by pets

languishing on inkless printers and crashed computers

I intend to inspire, mold, and scold

until they are responsible, respectful, life-long learners

who take joy in their creativity,

relish curiosity

and can conduct themselves compassionately.

And I hope to get to it all soon

Real soon

'Cause time's a wasting

and who knows…

It could be fun.

Poems For Oral Presentation

Throughout the creation of student poetry, it's important that the poems be heard. I suggest alternating between the teacher reading the students' work and the students reading their own poems or the poems of their peers. Poetic presentations also make for a wonderful culminating activity or parents' night performance. There are many ways to present the poems: solos, duets, small group choral readings and the incorporation of dance and music. Experimentation is the key. Perhaps small groups of students could be assigned to choreograph the same poem and then one group could be chosen to incorporate many of the ideas each group came up with. Be the poems serious or funny, here's wishing you fun with it all.

<u>Share This</u>

Peace is the word: spread it.

Hope is the feeling: share it.

Anger is the curse: end it.

Hunger is the need: feed it.

Love is the answer: live it.

Thesaurus Poem

I would be happy…no

Cheerful…no

    Delighted to have you by my side

But you're not here
          You're absent
            You're missing

I eagerly await your arrival

        Your entrance

        Your appearance

But I'm fearfully afraid that you may not show at all
    And then you'll never see my loving loyalty
        And dedicated devotion

And I would be hurt…
    No, wounded
        No, broken…hearted.

Kitchen Table Ring Side Seat

Sitting beside my fool friend
        Playing Monopoly for blood and money
                And then…
            Sirens passed by and she said
            "They're coming to get you."

    I later tore myself away from bankruptcy and bagels
And went walking into what a poet might call
            A quiet night

That's when the light
    Hit behind my right shoulder
                Circled on the trees and houses
                    As the wrecker passed by
            Dragging behind its baggage
                 So completely crumbled
    Scraping steel in a song across the pavement

But there are no pretty images to describe death

    They came to get me…
                        and missed

Excuses, Excuses

(inspired by a poem by Shel Silverstein)

adapted by Rod Martin

Mom, I can't go to school and take my test
I think I better stay home and rest
Cuz I think I've got gangrene and malaria
And the mongoose mumps
The futts and cuts and mother goose bumps
My teeth are tight, my tongue is dry
And I can't see color through my right eye
My toes turned green and my knees are blue
It might be the Vesuvius bug or Tasmanian flu
My lymph nodes are swole up twice their size
And when I burp, I cross my eyes
I gasp, I giggle, I sneeze, I cough
I think my belly button's falling off
My ears hurt when I move my head
And I think my liver's lost or dead
My neck is sore, my foot bone's busted
And when it rains, my hair gets rusted
My elbow's crooked, my back is sore
I can't find my heart beat anymore

My brain is broke, my tummy's turned
I skinny dipped and my buns got burned
My temperature is one-oh-five
It's a wonder that I'm still alive
I've got psychosis neurosis and depressive confusion
Delusions, contusions and optical conclusions
My back bone pains me when I breathe or blink
I'm going deaf and my nose hairs stink
I'm hearing voices and seeing double
And my rheumatism's giving me trouble
I told my mom, I've got lots more excuses
if you'd care to stay
But she just smiled and walk away
Saying, "what a shame, oh, and by the way
I bet you forgot today is Saturday."

What Poet's Do

Oh, you know…
It may seem strange
The way I can rearrange words
To say something
Or nothing at all
Like scrawl on the wall if you will, and still,
The poet is free
No, I will not be confined by my commentary
Absolutely unrestrained
I'm a run-away train
Not a trained little dog in a circus
Not the least bit bound
I speak for the sake of sound
Bursting around your ear-bones
Like headphones filled with rock and roll
An imaginary stroll on a tightrope of time
And nonsense and rhyme
Just for you

Because that's what poets do.

Understanding Poems

In relating to poetry,
whether you find it confusing…or not
You must see it and feel it, like a shivering hot
From the top of one's head, the words tumble down
Crumpled and broken and twisted around
Some slumping or soaring from tongue to mind's ear
A rhyme is developing, or so I do fear

Confined to a pattern? That's a waste of good time
Though darn it, the poem continues to rhyme
Now, let's have none of that. It's time to be free
And if you're following all this nonsense
you'll undoubtedly be
amused and confused cuz it's all clear as mud
Like a curtained metaphor night that falls with a thud

So much for symbolism, but keep it in mind
It's not hard to write poems

if you don't try to rhyme.

<u>Your heart is not a play thing</u>
A heart is not a toy,
But if you want it broken
Just give it to a boy
Boys like to play with things,
To see what makes them run
But when it comes to kissing
They do it just for fun
If you get a chance to see him
Your heart begins to dance
Your life revolves around him
There's nothing like romance
But boys never give their hearts away
They play us all for fools
They wait until we give them our hearts
And then they play it cool
After a while it starts to happen
You worry day and night
You wonder if you're losing him
It never turns out right
You may wonder where he is all day
You might wonder if he's true
One moment you'll be happy
The next moment you'll be blue
Boys are great, though immature
The price you pay is high,
He might seem sweet and gorgeous,
But remember, he's just a guy

Train whistle
A wisp of wind, chilly
Lamplight
A rich man passes a flower seller

>   A hard day, sir
>   So many flowers
>   A shame to see them wilt and die
>   Kind sir, buy a bit of love

A dollar changed hands

>   Kindled hope

The rich man caught his train

>   The flower man
>   bought the evening bread

He gave the flowers to the doorman
His daughter disliked flowers
Disliked her home
Her father's money
Herself

>   The flower family
>   Bent over the bread
>   Giving thanks

"Your wife's at bridge, sir
And young Freddie called
Said something about needing
More money for school
Will that be all, sir?"

>   After dinner, he told them tales
>   Of snow topped mountains
>   Then it's off to bed

Two martinis
And it's awful to be
Or was it three?

>   Say your prayers
>   And sweet dreams kids
>   I love you so

Another day, another dollar
Poor rich man

Love

Love is special
I share my love with a wonderful person
Building her dreams with my two hands
Each day learning, growing
showing how you are so special to me
Love is respect
Showing you how very sorry I am
when I do something wrong
Being willing to change
Love is responsibility
Working to keep the relationship going
no matter what happens
Love is painful at times,
Knowing how to keep my distance and let things cool off,
if I've made you mad.
Love isn't easy at all
But with you, it's worth every moment
or tear

The same?

(two students stand stuck back to back)

She: We're the same as you can see
He: I'm part of her and she's part of me
She: I want to live my life upon the stage
He: Well, I think night clubs are the rage
She: Oh, sure, you'd rather dance and sweat
He: It beats being bloody like Lady MacBeth.
She: Now, let's not argue, there are peopke here
He: Sorry, I didn't mean to upset you, dear
She: He's always the one to start a fight
He: So that's your game is it? Well, all right!
She: Please hold still. Don't make a fuss.
He: You're the one embarrassing us
She: That's just like you, the first to blame
He: As if you never do the same
She: Ok, you go your way, I'll go mine
(they're still stuck back to back)
He: You see, this happens every time
She: We really should learn to get along
He: You don't say. What are we doing wrong?

First Love

Isn't it funny how close we got?
How I could just be myself around you?
How you became my everything?
My love
My life
My partner in crime
My teddy bear when I need a hug
I thought we were perfect
And meant to be
The way you made me laugh
You made it seem like there were no worries in life and the
only thing that existed was me and you
I regret our fights
Our arguments
Our distrust
I wish we could have avoided the yelling
If we both learned to stop being jealous
The world could be jealous of us
If we learned to not have to have the last word, our last words
would have been "I love you."

Houseless

Is there homework for the homeless?

Do they share the same chores?

What's to sweep if you have no floors?

No indoors?

How can you write with no pen?

Why use deodorant when you can't find a shower?

Where do you hang your toothbrush in a public bathroom?

If you change clothes outside
Will you be scolded, or arrested or worse?

Maybe their homework is to find a home
Find a job

Stay alive

And maybe

Just maybe

We should help them too.

Catch Me Should I Break

I'm weak in my bones
    I'm weak because my heart can't escape life's torment.
      I'm weak in my wings, I need to fly.
      If only darkness could be washed away with tears;

Maybe I'd see heavenly sights,
    Maybe I'd find what I'm capable of being.
      Maybe I'd find out how beautiful my wings will be
        in the sun's light

If only, if only, time wasn't a puzzle.

Maybe I am weak in my bones,
    Maybe it's time I drop to my knees
      And let my heart begin beating in dark colors

If only, If only…

God, I know You're waiting for the day
    I surrender myself to you.

God, I know you're ready
    To catch me should I break.

And God, I know You know
    my wings are beautiful.

      If only, If only….

When Words Fail

When words fail, music speaks
Expressing all the shades of emotion one can portray

Nothing can compare with what's within the heart
It's what twinkles with sound

So, you can write with a bleeding pen
Or you can write with an imaginative mind
      It doesn't matter

Music conquers all when it's yours

It will forever be there
      and it will always allow you to stand tall

Rejoice in what you hear
      Put spirit into sound

      Make it you

What you speak can define what others hear

Keep it to yourself
      or be an open book
            willing to be read

When words fail, music speaks

FORGET HIM

FORGET HIS NAME, FORGET HIS FACE

FORGET HIS SMILE, FORGET HIS EMBRACE

FORGET THE TIMES THAT YOU ONCE SHARED

FORGET THE FACT THAT HE ONCE CARED

FORGET THE TIMES SPENT ON THE PHONE

FORGET THE TIMES YOU WERE ALL ALONE

FORGET THE TIMES YOU SPENT TOGETHER

REMEMBER HE'S GONE FOREVER

FORGET THE WAY HE LOVED YOU

FORGET THE WAY HE SPOKE TO YOU

REMEMBER NOW THERE'S SOMEONE NEW

AND DON'T FORGET, HE DEPENDS ON YOU

I'VE GOT AIDS?

I'VE GOT AIDS
I DON'T BELIEVE IT

I'VE GOT AIDS
WHAT WILL PEOPLE THINK OF ME?

I'VE GOT AIDS
NOW, I'M GOING TO DIE YOUNG

I'VE GOT AIDS
WILL EVERYONE STOP LOVING ME?

I'VE GOT AIDS
I FEEL UNCLEAN
OUTCAST

CONTAGIOUS

SCARED

'SAFETY FIRST' WAS THE LAST THING

ON MY MIND

HE WALKS ALONE

NO HOPE
NO FUTURE
NO HOME

SURVIVING ON DREAMS IN HIS HEAD
SOMETIMES HE'D RATHER BE DEAD

AND THEN A SMILE PASSES THROUGH
HIS TORMENTED LIFE
HER LAUGHTER SHINES IN THE LIGHT

AND HE DARES TO DREAM
OH, WHAT THAT MEANS!

HER BRIGHT HOPE ILLUMINATING
AND ELIMINATIING
HIS PAIN AND DISPAIR

CAN HE SHOW HER HE CARES?

OR WILL HE
SIMPLY
DISSAPPEAR INTO THIN AIR?

<u>Joy</u>

Happiness feels like new clothes out of the dryer.

It's like opening presents you always wanted.

It sounds like Christmas morning
    Crinkle, crumple, ripping of wrapping paper.

The oven timer beeping to say
    "The pie is done!"

Happiness wears bright colors.

It's a cool swimming pool
    on a hot day.

Happiness, stops by to say,

"I love you, don't ever go away
    and I will give you
        joy."

A BROKEN HEART

IS LIKE A CHILD'S TOY
LYING IN THE GUTTER
BY THE SIDE OF THE ROAD

A SHATTERED MIRROR
REFLECTING BROKEN HOPES

IT'S USELESS AS A PEANUT BUTTER AND JELLY
SANDWICH DROPPED IN THE SAND

IT HURTS LIKE A KID WITH A CUT FINGER

IT'S MUSIC WITHOUT MELODY, EMPTY

A RUSTED FERRIS WHEEL
UNABLE TO MOVE

AN EXPIRED COUPON

A BOUNCED CHECK

A NEWSPAPER LEFT IN THE RAIN

BUT MOSTLY, IT'S PAIN

So When Tomorrow Starts Without Me

When tomorrow starts without me

  and I'm not there to see

If the sun should rise and find

your eyes filled with tears for me,

I wish so much you wouldn't cry

  the way you did today

while thinking of so many things

  we didn't get to say.

I know how much you love me,

  as much as I love you.

And each time that you think of me

I know you miss me too.

But when tomorrow starts without me,

Please try to understand

that Jesus came and called my name

and took me by my hand,

and said my place was ready in heaven far above.

And I will have the comfort of living is His love

So when tomorrow starts without me,

don't think we're far apart

For every time you think of me,

I'm right here in your heart.

GOLDEN GLOVES

STICK

MOVE

JAB

LEFT HOOK

RIGHT HOOK

UPPERCUT

BODY BLOW

DUCK

RIGHT CROSS

KNOCK OUT
CHEERS!

BLOOD

BOXING

Tears Will Dry

One wish keeps you trying
Looking for that silver lining
You can fall a thousand times
Feeling like you've lost your mind
But love will find a way

We can all learn to love again
Trust again
Our hearts will mend
Tears will dry
We will survive

It only takes a moment to change your life

Only a dream to keep you wondering

Only a little love to light your way

Come and See

SUN SHOWERS AND RAINBOWS
THE BEAUTY HAWAII HOLDS

NO OTHER PLACE CAN COMPARE
TO THESE ISLANDS

LUSH MOUNTAIN VALLEYS
SYMPHONIES OF BIRD SONGS

PALM TREES SWAYING IN THE BREEZE
ON A SUNNY DAY
WHALES BURSTING FROM THE SEA IN PLAY

WATERFALLS STREAMING
DOWN HIGH MOUNTAINS

SEA BIRDS SOARING
ABOVE OFF SHORE ISLANDS

THE SUN SETS SO BEAUTIFULLY
COME VISIT US, YES COME AND SEE

Siamese Cat

Ice crystal eyes
Shining in the moon's light

Slick as silk
Reflected in a pond

Whiskers glow of silver
Stars twinkle above
As the snow begins to fall

Alone with the moon she walks
Shedding just for show

Curled up in a ball
Fading like the snow
With the moon's light

Beautiful creature of the night

YOU'RE MY FRIEND

BECAUSE YOU DON'T DROOL WHEN YOU TALK
LIKE MY COUSIN

AND YOU DON'T SMELL
AS BAD AS MY DOG

OR EAT LIKE A PIG

OR ATTRACT FLIES LIKE A COW

OR SAY STUPID THINGS ABOUT MY MOTHER

OR FORGET WHAT I TELL YOU

YOU'RE NOT AS DUMB AS MOST PEOPLE

OR AS UGLY AS SOME I'VE SEEN

AND THAT'S WHY I LOVE YOU

LIKE A FRIEND

Indian

Cherokee

    Victors of Wounded Knee

Indian Heart
    Tribal Pride
        People of the mountain side

Eagle feathers
    Leather thongs
        Healing chants and ancient songs

You may take this land from me
    And impose your cultural captivity

        But my eagle heart flies forever free

Do it All

I'm very competitive
When it comes to football

I wanna catch it
I wanna run it
I wanna do it all

I wanna score every point
I wanna hear the crowd scream

I wanna be a superstar
And fulfill all my dreams

And when I die, when comes my time

When I get to heaven,

I wanna be first in line.

Let Love Grow

Love is a flower

So let it bloom

Plant the seed

And give it room

Believe in the flower

Without any doubt

Water it daily

And watch it sprout

Be gentle and patient

And take it slow

And you will see how beautiful

Love will grow

Let me tell you why Hawaii's Cool

It's always nice

Not too hot or too cold

Beaches are cool

The women are beautiful

And the mountains are tall and green

The sky is pretty with trade wind breezes

The ocean is a wonderful playground

To surf and swim

Dive and fish

Boat and float

The valleys unspoiled by houses etc.

Living in harmony

Feels like paradise

to me

Let it be

I'm a Movie Man

Give me big screen theatres

with action movies

I'm talkin' fast cars and fast money

I feel like it's me up there on the screen

Know what I mean?

My car, my race, zooming by

crossing the finish line

nitros oxide speed

All I need is some action

Winning the race

crossing the line

winning the gold

the trophies

ribbons and more

All the girls knocking on my door

here to celebrate my race

congratulating me

by kissing my face

Hatred

Hatred burning inside us
Raging fury
Some hold it in, some let it out
Good? Bad?
Hurts you to hold it in
Hurts others to let it out
Like a raging father disciplining his son
A hit to the gut
Some embrace it, others hate it
Hatred kills you inside
Caused by jealousy, fear, sometimes love
You can never predict what may happen
You wear a mask, killing your victims
Some may ask "why?" Why are you here?
Why must this happen?
Hurting, destroying
I want you gone, out of my life
So, I take a stand. You cannot control me!
I rule my world. Know that now!
Hatred, be gone!

Imagine With Me

Imagination leads your mind to explore

    You can visit exotic places or visit the deepest depths of the sea

        who knows where you will be?

Your mind can take you where you never thought you'd go

    It can dress you up and put on a spectacular show

Once you start who knows where you'll end up?

    No limits. No bounds. Like the constant flow of the ocean

      If there's a thousand people, there could be a thousand dreams

Who can dream of flying? You can!

    Your arms become wings and your body, weightless

        lifting off the ground feeling the breeze in your face

          Imagination can take you a long, long way

    As long as you set your mind to it

      your imagination will do it

Creation

Multiplication, makes my head split.

Aggravation, someone's gonna get hit!

Motivation, helps you do your best.

Relaxation, helps you get your rest.

Cooperation, we're all one team!

Meditation, helps you dream.

Creation, like the stars above.

Imagination, see the things you love.

Consideration, being so nice.

Recommendation, you should take my advice.

Medication, you'll feel better.

Notification, by e-mail or letter.

Communication, you can speak your heart.

Education, that's were it starts.

Participation, that's doing things with friends.

Anticipation, I wonder how this poem ends....

Where I Left My Legs

Nobody asked me to go to war

I felt I had to go

And if I was going to die

I knew all of my family would cry

Now, I wonder who will wonder, "why?"

Was it worth the sacrifice?

Fighting for freedom in this foreign land

    where I left my legs behind

        I still don't understand

On Two Wheels

Jumping ramps in the hot sunshine

    having fun and feeling fine

racing my friends feels like flying

    I may not win but I sure am trying

speeding around the track

    how good it feels

the most fun a guy can have on two wheels

Ho Hum, Here It Comes

School's boring

like corn flakes with no sugar

watching grass grow

more boring than watching my mom sleep

or watching paint drying

or an unplugged TV

And so my friend

this poem must end

because you see

it's boring me.

Candyland

What if the world was candy?

The ocean would be like Jello

Like when you climb the tree and pick the

leaves you get licorice

And the mud is one hundred percent pure chocolate fudge

The paper would be like fruit roll ups

The sand would be small sugar sprinkles

Then the walls would be like Hersey squares at Waikiki

And the glass windows would be sugar

Then when you walk down the stairs it's like wafers

People everywhere made of starburst

and rocks are sour skittles

Back To The Past

If I went back in the past

I would like to go back to where my Dad was killed.

If I was there I could have prevented that from happening.

I could have saved him.

If I did save him then our family would have been perfect.

But I can't stop him from dying

because it was his destiny.

It was the plan that God made for him.

It is impossible to change God's decision.

If I can't save him from dying

then I want to go back

and spend the last moment with my Dad.

I want to play with him,

laugh with him and kiss his cheek.

Feel his warm arms holding me so lovingly and gently.

Remembering the best moment in my life.

seeing makes me happy

seeing makes me sad

seeing confuses everything

seeing makes me mad

seeing is depressing, yet

seeing is so sweet

seeing is heart wrenching, but

seeing makes me weak

seeing is to live

living is to see

let not love disappear

for seeing is to be

do you know what's going on? Are you one of the few?

'cause now I'm awfully fond of seeing

and what I see is you

<u>Let me tell you it hurts</u>

when someone breaks your heart

or when they say those cruel words

and words tear you apart

It hurts when your parents don't care

when everyone stares

it hurts in the bottom of my soul

yes, it takes its toll

It hurts to be lied to your face

you feel so disgraced

Let me tell you it hurts

to feel so alone

no e-mails or messages

a silent phone

I'm not one to hold grudges

But in a world where everyone judges

Let me tell you it hurts.

Why People Live...

Love is why people live
It's everywhere
It's powerful
Wonderful
Unbreakable
Unique
Patient
Serious
It's respect and honesty
And it's made for everyone

Love is gentle
It's when you like being around someone
Spending time with them
Believing
Being there for someone
Caring about others
Making people feel good
Compromising, compassion and
Caring for something other than yourself
Giving money to a good cause

Spending time with family
It's why people smile
Trusting one another
Being able to speak your heart

Love is heartbreaking
Confusing
Depressing

Love is willing to let go
More ups and downs than a roller coaster
Not getting your own way
Love is hard

Love is trusting and
Beautiful
Tenderness and
Happiness
Time together
Joyful Affection
It's what gives people butterflies

It's awesome
Priceless
The best

It's a strong, crazy, wonderful thing
Full of surprises

It's unexplainable
Special
Worth living for

It keeps the world together

<u>Like oxygen…</u>

Love is a cornucopia of feelings
        for a special someone

Love is whatever you want it to be

Love is…
Giving
Caring
Something everyone needs, like oxygen

Love is great
Beautiful
Enjoyable
Valuable
Powerful
Wonderful
Special
Timeless
Forever
Love is like you're in heaven

Love is giving someone your heart
It's romantic
Holding hands
Hugs
Kisses
Cupid
Chocolate

Flowers
Cuddling
Showing how you feel
Expressing affection
Long walks at sunset
Like floating on cloud nine
Dedicating yourself
Marriage
Love never leaves you

Love is the best thing in the world
It's truthful
Patient
Faithful
Pure
Kind
Trustworthy
Healing

It's happiness
It's fun

Love is confusing
Love is good, most of the time
Love is strong
Love lifts us up
It's a treasure in our hearts

Its responsibility
A commitment
Being open
Love is friends and family

Love is something scientists can't explain

Love keeps us together

With love you can't be lonely

Love is complicated

Love is giving someone the ability to hurt you
        but trusting them not to
It's pain, sometimes
Tears
Letting go
Love is not a game

Love is better than hate

It's awesome
Wild
Magnificent
Exciting
Outgoing
Doing crazy things
You can't over-love someone

Love is something you'll never forget

Love is something you can't live without

Love is hope for peace on earth

My Inspiration

I am my own self

My own transformation

I know how to use my imagination

I go to school for education

Spend my time in observation

I have determination

motivation

You might say my mom's my inspiration

that's why I show her appreciation

I tip toe during her meditation

Help do dishes so she can have some relaxation

It doesn't feel like an obligation

If you need further explanation

I'd say, "that's what love looks like"

In way of illustration.

Why do we lie?
Why are boys dirty?
Why are girls clean?
Why do we scream?
Why is the sky blue?
Why isn't it green?
Why do dogs bark?
Why can't I be seen?
Why do we love?
Why is this so?
Why do birds fly?
Why don't we know?
Why are there back-stabbers?
Why does it hurt?
Why do we part?
Why do we flirt?
Why are we here?
Why can't we fly?
Why do we fight?
Why do people get high?
Why are bones hard?
Why can't they bend?
Why don't I continue?
Because this is the end!

Mall-ation

The following is my shopping
Information
Since the mall is my favorite
Destination
It's not a chore, it's more like a
Vacation
So many things in so many stores
Fascination
But when its crowded like Christmas
Aggravation
Check out the food court, that's my
Recommendation
My savings account is my only
Limitation
It hard to pay those credit card
Obligations
And just window shopping is such a
Frustration
I want to own stuff, not just use my
Imagination

If It Takes a Lifetime

Sometime

In your lifetime

Something opens your eyes

To the love

All around you

And you realize

That if it takes a lifetime

Then how lucky you'll be

And you can love those around you

Yes, love sets you free.

<u>Check out this communication situation</u>

I pose to those this dedication
this cooperation of information and inspiration
which is an indication of the power of transformation
An illustration of articulation
unbound by punctuation

I present a proclamation revelation
for your consideration

"There's an explanation for every destination."

For further clarification and/or interpretation
of this conversation
I leave you with this quotation:

"May your participation
in the exploration of further education
provide sufficient stimulation of your imagination."

<u>Betty Sue</u>

Betty Sue of Tuskaloo
Walks along the railroad tracks
That pass through her small town

Looking down and remembering the young man, Dan
Who passed through her life
      Her town
      Her love

He came to build a school
He left to fight a war a world away

And when came the day
That train brought him back
As he stood there beside the track
Betty Sue instinctively knew
That the love she once had come to know
Had died in a battle not so long ago

And only a body here remained
To carry around the living pain
Like the lonesome moan of a passing train

Optimism

What does optimism mean?

It means to keep on hopin'
    when others aren't copin'.

To see the beauty around you.

To see the humor in life and to laugh often.

To dream a future, remembering the past, grounded in the present moment.

To be the kind of person who looks for the loving thing to do and say.

It means staying positively positive.

To keep on going and growing and trying and learning and turning the world on its ear.

We need more optimism around here.

A Few Moments More

Seconds race by
Human race by the time our day is done
            we fall at the feet of forever
            begging for but a few moments more

    'til…

        BANG goes the gun
                Off at a run
Chasing each moment by racing each moment

            And it's gone

        No time to mourn it
From the day you're born it's a contest with time

        Find the reason, the rhyme
Though you run 'til you ache with each step you take

            Desiring it
            Expiring it

Each second you take up
Can never be made up
So cherish your space in the race

<u>We think we're so great</u>

because we create

But wait…

Humpback whales also create

Their songs

Most human kind songs are long gone

Swallowed by history

Not matter…the importance is song

And getting along

Like harmony

Would whales wage war under the sea?

Wouldn't that be a silly thing

when it's so much more fun…to sing.

What is Truth?

What if truth?

     Who's to say?

Can truth, like man, pass away?

    If the word were carved in stone

       Mountain Big and in a line

         Doesn't stone wear to dust

           amid the test of time?

Wishes

Don't wish upon a falling star

    Or set your hopes on a heaven far

When love's the key to paradise

    And peace on earth

        Let love suffice.

Some say the world will end in fire
And some say ice

Frost said, from what he'd tasted of desire
He held with those who favor fire

But if it had to perish twice

    We all know enough of hate

To say that for destruction

    Ice is also great

        And would suffice

Inhale

Every breath

    Every conscious breath

        Can be a meditation, of sorts

            Sniffs and snorts of mother air

Which we hardly appreciate

    Until it's not there for a minute or two

If only our love for each other

    Could become as indispensable

        As air.

Sand

Sand is more
      Than something that sneaks
              Into sneakers
     Is sifted through fingers
    Plastered in castles
It is a massive amount of water
           Showing boulders who's boss
    The futile battle of stone to remain together
It's a highway at low tide
   A moving hill
       Jogging path and moldable bed
     Young minds museum playground
It's little chunks of rock, coral and shells
     And other erosion resistant minerals
It's crunchy in oatmeal
     Palatable on peanut butter and jelly
       Not so spicy in soup
But basically, it's all over everything
              at the beach
it's amazing
it's where sea kisses earth
union
shifting alliances and illusions

the softest of stone

Shark Park

Ever take a walk through Shark Park?
Seaweed greenery
On coral kingdom scenery
But beware of visits at dark

The king of that scene
Fast swimming and lean
Has only one thing on his mind

To hunt, always seek
Something easy to eat
Now, isn't it past dinner time?

Night strolls could cost you dear
The kings of Shark Park rule here.

Mosquito

Poor little mosquito

    He's drawn his last breath

    For he

        Who bites me

        Tastes death.

<u>Life's Intersections</u>

Life presents us with many paths

Intersection decisions

Roadblock frustrations

Dead end relationships

Stoplight procrastinations

Speeding dreams

Fender bender love affairs

Down-hill illnesses

And too soon

Exits

Someone To Hold You

Never forget

    no matter how big you've grown

        that you began life's journey as a babe

           who couldn't have survived alone

And though you speak in learned circles

    with the knowledge of your years

        your first utterances were babble

           punctuated by tears

no matter how self-sufficient you feel

    or what others may have told you

        just as in your beginning

           you still need someone to hold you

Most Alone

The most alone thing

Is waking up

To the same thing you saw

When you went to sleep

And it only has one eye

That cannot see you, you see?

It's your TV.

A Broken Heart

A broken heart is like a night with no stars

Or going to the prom with your mom

It's a shattered window that lets in the cold

The sound of old love songs

played through blown out speakers

It's a guitar with no strings, no song to play

A pain, like cancer

A fever everyone fears to touch

Oh yes, a broken heart can hurt that much

Strawflower Expectations

Crushed
> Like a flower

Pressed
> Between the pages of my own aching

Shattered
> By the breaking of my hope

Strawflower expectations
> Having lost their living luster

Dried up
> Finding no comfort from rain-like tears
> > Which don't
> > > Which I won't let flow

First flower of loving

Plucked

Pressed

Unable to grow

Love Is All

Love is all I have to give you

Love is all I have to give

Love is all I have

Love is all

Love is

You

<u>Wire and water.</u>
Those are the questions.
Why are we here?
What are we supposed to be doing?
What are our chances?
Why are we waiting?

Life's full of questions.
Can be full of love, which is the answer
The solution
Forgiveness
Hope
Love that brings joy in the giving

Wire and water.
Why are we here?
To Love

Water.
What are we waiting for?
Wire
Why are we so dumb?
In a life too short for hate and hurt.

What are we waiting for?
Today's the day.
The start of all the love you can hold in your heart.
Wire and water.

Shout This Poem

I travel at the speed of poetry

Moving though time

Free

To rhyme of ramble

I roam about

I sing this poem

I laugh

I shout this poem to the stars

Such sweet release

A poem for peace

In this world of ours.

Baby's Day

Hey little one, how was your day?
Too young to crawl, to draw, to play.
What did you do girl, give me the scoop?
"Same as yesterday, eat, sleep and poop."

Just a few weeks old and cute as a button.
Don't tell me you just lazed around
Not doin' nothing.
Did you learn new things?
Make memories to keep?
"Hard to say when you just
poop, eat and sleep."

Well, you just keep on growing
You've got all the time in the world
We love just to watch you and hold you
You're such a good girl
It's a wonderful world
With so many nice people to meet
But for now little girl
You just poop, sleep and eat.

First Times

The first time ever I heard silence
    Not that the world stood still
        But it was the right kind of noise

Early morning river rapids
    And the sound of sunshine through branches

I stretch in my homemade hammock
        A drowsy rebirth

Yes, I've tasted freedom
And heard the way the world wakes in the morning

I've lived close to the earth
        Like a river
    With a feeling of flowing

            Knowing why I'm here

And the silence
        For once
            Was inside me

Political Hold Out

Whether you've declared yourself
    Democrat
    Republican
    Independent
    Uninspired or otherwise

Hold out
    Hoping for the day you'll vote through your TV

When the land of the free
    A government of the people and for the people
        Will ask the people to have a hand and a say

Hold out
    Hoping for the day
When we'll quit worrying why everything's a mess
    And start taking a guess at a better way

      Hold on

      Hold out for the day

Yesterday's Melodies

How can I face today
    When yesterday's melodies
        Are all I seem to remember?

Sweet September love songs
    And October walks in harmony

Your November embrace
    And Christmas kisses

New years' nonsense
    February's fight
The reconciliation of March
    April's shower of tears

May I see you agains
    And June weddings forsaken

July's sad music of missing
    The sweaty blues of summers end

You sing a song of separation to me now
    Such a cool tune

Alone

Alone in my head
    On no one's mind
Do I exist?

    My name
        On pieces of paper

            In files, on lists, exists
        Pieces of paper exist

Writing this poem
    Black ink on off-white paper
        Poem exists

I'm a tree falling in a forest
    (trees fall to become paper)
        with no one to hear the sound
I don't care
    This tree exists

    Alone in this forest
        This room
            My head

Writing this poem

On no one's mind

I don't care, I exist

A word called caring

Written in black ink

Though writing doesn't make it real

I don't care

I do care
I exist

Even if no one hears, I exist

Even if no one cares, I exist

Someone, someday, will care, I hope.

Safe From Harm

Snowed in

outside the window
blowing
snowing
and knowing
you're snowed in

drifting

sifting

and uplifting

to be close and warm
safe from harm

Sparkler Boy

Perhaps I might

    Pass death by

And forsaking heavenly custom,

      Melt into cool laser light

        Flowing into patterned colors

          Black space

            And shining stars

      The beauty that is being

      A child playing with light

        At night

The Tale of the Vorple Snit

Once upon a flip flop
There lived a Vorple Snit
Who rode a fransome gopler
And spoke with words of glit
But a fierce and flying krunster
Brought terror to the land
And all the folks of frick frack said
Someone must take a stand!
Fear not, you pluffer gunkles
Said the fearless Vorple Snit
I shall face that flying krunster
And I'll glip it where it flits
Twas a fierce and noshous battle
With fire and screams and slopter
But victory came at last
To the Vorple Snit atop his fransome gopler
And now, throughout the land
Glimsome songs are heard
All hail the Vorple Snit
Who saved us by his bravery and glerd.

Money

Well, you talk about income
I'd sure like some
A little dough don't you know
and I could get down
but there's just not enough green stuff around
I've got a coupon, can I win that prize
At your bargain basement computer compromise
You got a sale I can save on everything I see
Just like the garbage on my home TV
You know I wanna buy it all
though it's working me dead
I'm a TV kid with a TV head
Yes, I sit up with my set
in the middle of the night
Just to fall asleep by the TV light
Then I wake up in the morningr
To the news each day
And they say everything's a mess
And it'll never go away
And I get deeper in debt brother every day

Chinkle chankle, I'd like a whole bank full
I'd be so thankful, yea, for some money

Raisin' my rent, my money's spent
I hear there's war in the government
I'm hopin' for a settlement
I don't need napalm, A-bombs or H-bombs
Battleships at sea or missiles over me
I'm in love with my life
And I'm happy just to live
And if I had money, no, I wouldn't give it
To blowin' things up or tearin' things down
Listen children, what's that sound?
Everybody gotta stop what's goin' down
With your money, cuz it's your money
Your money
Gotta tell those boys
That the price of their toys is too high to pay
And everyone,
everywhere, everyday needs money
There's sure a lot of rich people I know
Got more than they need
But they'd never let it go
Now, why don't they share some
It's only fair to spare some money for the people
We're talkin' board and bread
And you can't take it with you brother
                when your dead.
        It's only money.

Forget Love

You can pray and preach
            Bow and chant
                        Meditate and contemplate
            But don't forget love
You can climb mountains
      And sit surrounded by bird song breezes
            But please, don't walk away from love
You can talk to your friends
      e-mail everyone you know
      bounce ideas off satellites in space
      but don't forget to mention love wins
You can be rich and famous
            Envied and pampered
                        Able to buy a slice of paradise
But my advice is to spend some time
            Looking for the loving thing

            Then sing, dance, sculpt, write
      and try to create more love
wherever you go
      however much you can
            no matter what you do
                  don't forget to love.

Hey Kids, Listen Up

I write this to read this to you kids to say
    I'm thankful you're here, kids
           This could be the day
    I reach you and teach you
         to find your own voice
    You've got the chance
   You make the choice
There's a world of ideas
      bouncing 'round in your head
and when you write them down, so they can be read
then others might know what you're feeling inside
and they too will write
    and then know the pride
       of sharing a moment
          or speaking their heart
Just a pencil on paper
      That's where it starts
There's a kind of magic
The way words paint a scene
Do you get the picture?
   Do you understand what I mean?
There's a joy to creating
        To making something new
I hope you'll enjoy writing
      Because it's part of you.

Why? Right?

Why write?

Why bother to compose
    this poetry or prose?

Hasn't somebody said it all before?

How can there be more to say?

And who would listen, anyway?

Might as well hang this poem up to dry

And never ask a poet, "Why?"

Long Live Liberty

We the people
The American masses
The hippies, rich dudes
Preachers and pacifists
Rednecks and nudists
Indians and engineers
Together
We determine what it means to be
The land of the free
Us athletes and welfare mothers
Old folks and astronauts
Farmers and free thinkers
Cub scouts and drop outs
Prisoners and pioneers
We each make up America the beautiful
    And each
        In his and her own way
            Define and defend
            Freedom for all.

<u>Flat on my Amsterdam back</u>

with a window to the world above

And a serenade of sky

A sentence of serenity

Punctuated by birds

Wishing they could nest near the warmth
of my window

There are dots of dirt on the glass

and specks of dust on my spectacles

The only imperfections between me

and an afternoon aftermath of a rainy day

turned cloudless blue

a light blue

Sunlight through Dutch window

Such a view

No Better Way to Be

If ever the government
        Federal
                State
                        Judicial

Authorities that be
        Try to tell me
                I cannot be free
                        As I see fit
                                Then that's it

I will gladly return all the little plastic cards
                        papers and passwords
                    numbers and networks
                all ID that dares define me

    and they can come find me in the hills

            waking to the birds
                    far away from the words: do dis and dat

            When one lives free
                    there seems no better way to be.

Young

    Growing old

        I should be worried, or so I'm told

Yet I'm still young, and worries I lack

    I'm just glad I'm not old, looking back…

Wrapped in a warm blanket of memories
            Forgotten
              Forgiven
  A wavering mind
    Years gone by
Surely I can remember if I try

Huddling in this blanket because I'm always cold

No,

I'm glad I'm still young, just growing old

What is Light?

The fastest of dreams
      The beams that streak through endless night
         The light of stars

          The light within
            that hides/resides inside us all

Refracted rainbows bright
       Creator's colors
         Captured in flowers
         Envied by artists

It's the warmth,
     the love that burns and turns the world
         separating day from night
             Sweet sunlight

And at life's end
     this shining friend is there to guide us
         into a whole new way of being
    and it will be alright
         Trust in the light

Someone once said,

"Your heart is dead."

And that's why I'm living...

scared.

Manipulator

Me, the manipulator
I begin to see it
Rarely control it
Often deny it
Haven't perfected it
Wish I could stop it
Doubt that I need it
Enjoy when I do it
Know where I learned it
Know why I use it
Maybe I should

Quit.

In closing

I am the poem and the poem is me

       Free!

If you write about nothin'

            nothin's what you get

      'cuz nothin' comes from nothin'

      at least it hasn't yet

You'll just be spinnin' your wheels

      and you know how that feels

Too much head and not enough heart

Too soon it ends, it all depends

      on what you say at the start

Nothin' ventured, nothin' gained, nothin' left to do

The only thing that matters at all is you.

What is Truth?

If truth is being right

    From which perspective should we look

        And not be blinded by biased light

And if the word "Truth" were carved in stone

    Mountain high and in a line

        Remember stone still turns to dust

        Amidst the test of time.

My Answer

With whom do I live?

To whom do I give

All my love and affection?

To whom every poem?

My heart?

My home?

My answer is you.

V-Ball

Bump, Set, Slam, Dig
    Wahine Volleyball is very big.

    Just ask the crowds
        Who wait in line.
Just ask that darling girl of mine.

      Serve, Pass, Set, Kill

    Will they win?
        You know they will.

Dink, Dive, Shout, Scream!
    We support our Rainbow Team.

      Jump, Block, Roof, Cheers!
This could surely be our year.

Watch The Wave,

    Around it goes,

      Our way of saying

      Let's go Bows!

<u>Poem as Prayer, Not Out There</u>

Lord, the more I look

The more I find

Awaken my heart

Soothe my mind

Heighten my joy

Lower my pride

Be not, out there

Be here, inside.

Find Joy

Buy it, use it, break it, lose it. We consumers, we must choose it.

From phones to cars to candy bars.

We be eating, talking, driving.

We'll do anything to keep surviving.

Change it, rearrange it. Can't face it? Best erase it.

Computers, TVs, and other machines;

We rely on them more and more it seems.

Scrunch it, scoot it, better reboot it.

When technology fails, we still pursue it

Use your imagination to improve your situation.

Creativity can lead to innovation.

Don't succumb to the daily grind.

Find joy in each day and peace of mind.

Our legacy is not in our possessions.

It's in the memories of our life's sessions

Life is short, tell everyone, have some fun until it's done.

<u>Because I'm free</u>, it's not easy to describe me

I'm not lazy, I'm kick back

I'm not egotistical, just totally cool

I'm not bad, I'm rad

I'm not short, just vertically challenged

I'm not dumb, just not the sharpest shovel in the shed

I'm not stressed, just high strung

I'm no baby, just forever young

I'm not old fashioned, just proper

Not overly handsome, I'm no show stopper

Not a player, just a ladies man

Besides I'm still decidin' just who I'll be

and who I am.

So Many Are the Lemmings
(and so are we)

Humans

      Like Lemmings be

    We populate so proficiently

Now when do we begin

      our walk to the sea?

"Be fruitful and multiply"

      to fill the earth

    age after age

      birth after birth

We conquer the moon

      The land

      The seas

But will it end up standing room only, please

    Oh, why did we ever leave the trees?

A Bad Poem?

This is a bad poem
      the love in it is dried up
            the metaphor, ridiculous

       the similes are
                  bent
                     and broken

         the rhyme, non-existent

its helter skelter rhythm
      plays like burnt bongos

      the stanzas are
            slanted and silly

            and the whole kit and caboodle

                        ends abruptly

My Marvelous Mom

Great and glorious
Obviously excellent
Tremendously terrific and tender
Fabulous and fun
Amazingly awesome
Sensational and inspirational
You're a hard working woman
Witty, warm and wise
Neighborly and nice
Comforting, caring, kind
Thoughtful and thorough
Lovely and loving
Gentle, generous and genuine
Reliable and righteous
Humorous and humble
Considerate and compassionate
Fondly affectionate
Understanding, upstanding and outstanding
My marvelous Mother Dear

Walk, Man

Summer heat
City street

I boogie bounce by hustle and bustle
    And busses and cusses and traffic jam fusses
Wrapped in my I-pod, Walkman, Discman
      Security blanket of sound

I cruise this town
    Dancing and strolling
      Rocking and rolling

No, you can't say a word
    Not a one would be heard

Not a sad city thing
      As I strut like a king

On my musical mountain of sound

      Down town

AMERICA'S DIVERSITY

We the People,

Citizens of all backgrounds and creeds,

Uniquely different, yet Americans all the same.

Our love for our Country remains.

Long live liberty! Yes, liberty through diversity.

Us Athletes and Welfare Mothers,
       Old Folks and Astronauts,
              Farmers and Free Thinkers,
                     Cub Scouts and Drop Outs,
                            Prisoners and Pioneers.

We each make up America the Beautiful,
       And each, in his and her own way,
              Define and defend Freedom for All.

And it takes all kinds,
       All kinds of people,
              Each unlike any other,
                     Unique so to speak.

Expectant Mothers and Black Power Brothers,

Entertainers and Explainers, Teachers and Preachers.
Together, we determine what it means to be,
            the Land of the Free.
This Nation of Immigrants and Refugees,
        who have found a home, a safe place to be.

The Veterans and Pacifists,
        Scientists and Pessimists,
                Rednecks and Hipsters,
                    Indians and Engineers,
                        Toddlers and Smooth Talkers.

The Homeless and the Wealthy,
        The Sick and the Healthy,
                Introverts and Extroverts.

For all our quirks and imperfections,

        We're united in our shared affection,

            For this Country that we call Home,

                From sea to sea, with room to roam.

Us Writers and Fighters and Hikers and Bikers,
        Police with big sticks,
                Poets with word tricks.
                    Let's hear it for Converts and Convicts!

The Deaf, the Dumb, the Blind: all kinds!

Politicians! Morticians! Mormons on missions!

    Street Musicians to please us,
        Lawyers to squeeze us.

It astounds the imagination
    how many different minds and kinds of people
        it takes to make a Nation, this Nation.

So let's give thanks to the Men and Women
    who lay down their lives in war after war,
        no matter what those wars are for.

Give thanks to all those Nine-to-fivers,
    The Late Arrivers,
        The Holocaust Survivors,
            Who keep plugging away.
        Who are willing to pay
For our multiple sins, or our marvelous deeds.

God bless every Soul Searching Soul in need.

    Every Man, Woman, Boy and Girl,
        Who make this such an interesting World.

Someday There'll Be Love

We're going to put away the weapons
    With thanks to the TV
        Communication can cause changes
           Light illuminates, you see
And everybody's learning
    We get brighter all the time
And there will be a better day
    When we all start to shine
And the light is love. It's love

The world is more than nations
    Even nature's got a song
        And we could find a harmony
        When we lean to get along
Yes, I've seen it on my TV
    From a camera on the moon
        A brighter day, earth rising
           And it's coming just as soon
              Just as soon as we love.

So you keep on hoping for a brighter day
    And spread the news around
We're going to build a better world
    We're not going to tear it down'
We're going to be the kind of people
    to put an end to war
        and start to live our lives in love
           like we've never loved before
           let there be love.
              Yes, love.

Flutter-By

I wish I was a butterfly

And if you ever ask me "Why?"

I'd say, "I want to flutter by,

To fly on loving wings."

Yes, a Flutter-by in frolic flight

If wish you may, then wish you might

Wish for peace on earth

A peace so dear

Now look around.

It's here.

It's here.

Doctor Duke's Amazing Elixir of Life

Friends, and you are my friends
You seen it advertised on radio and TV, so it must be true
That Dr. Duke's Amazing Elixir of Life is modern medicine's
miracle answer to all your aches ailments and illnesses.

Yes, friends, whether you suffer from back-ache,
heart ache, halitosis or hemorrhoids,
Dr. Duke's will clear it up while it clears you out.

Safe enough for a baby baboon's bath water
Yet tough enough to knock out everything from dandruff to diarrhea!

It don't matter whether you're blind, bald-headed or brain-dead,
Dr. Duke's can help heal your stigmatism, rheumatism,
gas pains or pimples.

Just read the label: good for wheezin', sneezin', bedwettin' and warts,
coughs, colds, cancer and unsightly leg hair
.
Buy it by the case and say goodbye to the mumps, measles and malaria.

Feel free to use it liberally, internally, externally and eternally.

Finally a cure to ease the consternation of constipation.

And folks, I am livin' proof of its effectiveness
'cause I can tell you I have been drinkin' Dr. Duke's all day
and I swear, I am feelin' no pain.

Now who wants a bottle?

Babbling Barristers

The issue here is to hear the issue here
To which I'd like to object,
that is, if no one objects to my objection
And before we begin preliminary proceedings
and begin to start thinking about starting to begin,
I must point out that the preceding objection
misses the point made previously
off the recorded record.
And for the record, let me make it perfectly clear that the
statement I am about to make
is not an attempt to circumvent the issue
Even though what you may think I said
is not what I meant to convey
That is I think you misinterpreted
what I thought I said,
if I do indeed understand what you meant
by the afore mentioned statement.
I say this only to clarify
what has already been adequately conveyed
and to prevent confusion
rather than confound opposing counsel's conclusion.

Braggin'

I'm a good poet
    Well, not just good…
        And 'great' doesn't quite cover it
'Outstanding' comes close
    As does 'magnificent'
        Though I prefer 'unparalleled'.
(Most any superlative is always appreciated)
    Though I don't need others singing my poetic praises
        To maintain my sense of competent accomplishment
Frankly, words themselves fail to adequately describe
the poetic pinnacles of satiric success I have achieved,
        or so I believe
    Which is in itself ironic and a paradox
Since words themselves are the very tools I employ
    to express my thoughts,
        My emotions and memories,
    To describe life's mysteries,
    To analyze,
    And categorize,
    And dramatize
Each occurrence and endeavor that catches my fancy.

And though, it's true, I don't need the praise…
Yet, I humbly accept it
    As a necessary result
        Of unintended greatness on my part
When you honor me, you honor my art

It's Relative

Those who know

Plate tectonics

Tell me I'm movin' real slow

Don't they know
I really zippin' along
On a spinnin' world
Racing around the sun
In a rotating galaxy
That's flying through space?

It's a wonder

I'm not more tired

From keeping up

With such a pace

Just Say It Then

Just want to say
If you don't mind
Not to offend, mind you
Or appear politically incorrect
But I feel it must be said
And if no one else is going to do it
I'm more than willing
To step up to the plate
So to speak
So bear with me
For even though it seems obvious to some
It's worth hearing again and again
So I'm proud to say
Proud and honored to relate this simple truth
That covers a cacophony of sins

Love wins.

Poets Prayers

Now I lay me down to write

Before I go to sleep this night

If I should die before I wake

My penmanship's my least mistake

And now I sit me down to text

I have no idea what happens next

If I should die before it's sent

I hope someone wonders where I went

Poem About Love

I'm a poem about love.
　　Well, I'm not, but this is.
　　　　Will this be followed by a quiz?
A poem about love
　　　　and love's crazy phases
　　　　　　　　and phrases
　　　　　　and prolonged gazes through time
a poem about love and rhyme
　　a poem about two things at the same time

What I mean to say is,
　　What I'm trying to convey is,
　　　　The big thought for today is:
　　　　　　Love is more than a dream
　　　　More than part of the rhyme scheme,

But why should I philosophize
　　　　in a poem you won't bother to memorize
　　　　　　be we lovers or friends,

　　The point of this poem is,
　　　　　　unlike this poem,
　　　　　　　　love never ends.

<u>Nice Advice</u>

Show kindness

Stay humble

Express gratitude

Be courageous

Stay curious

Appreciate nature

Love unconditionally

Celebrate life

Be honest

Embrace change

Keep learning

Nurture relationships

Encourage others

Find Peace

Be patient

Laugh often

What She's Not

My girl is the best, yes she's really hot

But let me tell you what she's not. She's not lazy or crazy

Not catty or crude, lewd or rude

She's not overly proud or exceedingly loud

Nor does she stand out in a crowd

She's not mean or haughty, obscene or naughty

Not weird or flaky, though her self-esteem is a little bit shaky

She's not snide or stuck up inside,

No her actions are always dignified

She's perky and zealous but not petty or jealous

She's not saucy or bossy or greedy or needy

She's not in the way, never a problem

And never a pain in anyone's bottom

She's not flawed or odd

She's practically perfect

Just ask God

Rhyme Time

Poetry
Can really be
Done so easily

Poems are fun, like playing a game

There are so many words that sound the same

Rhyme for the challenge or to just pass the time

Make it silly or sassy as long as it rhymes

You can rhyme pickles with tickles

Or your toes with your nose

Try oodles with noodles and see how it goes

Try fish in a dish or flies in the skies

Hot dogs or bull frogs and hot apple pies

Nice dreams and moonlight

Ice cream and frostbite

Nothing to it, you can do it

You can rhyme first thing in the morning

Or on a lazy afternoon

You can turn it into a song if you can find a tune

Sing it, shout it, tell your friends all about it

Tell anyone near enough to hear the stuff

It's all about sound and things to say

You can do it

You'll find a way

Can a drizzle fizzle?

Do trees sneeze?

Does a stream dream?

Can the sky fly?

Rhyme high or rhyme low

Take a rhyme with you wherever you go

But you don't have to rhyme all the time

Still, when all is said and done, it can be lots of fun

Wishes

Don't wish upon a falling star

Or set your hopes on a heaven far

When love's the key to paradise

And peace on earth

Let love suffice.